"For decades John Perkins's footsteps have be
ity, like Moses. And Charles Marsh has been tracking those footsteps with·
the eye of a historian, showing us that this liberation journey is an ancient
one, and it ain't over yet. . . . It did not end with Moses or with Dr. King,
nor will it end with John Perkins. In *Welcoming Justice,* Perkins and Marsh
have created a perfect harmony, a freedom song that will echo with hope
through the streets of injustice and the halls of academia, inviting everyone
who hears to take a step out of the empire in which we live and to move one
step closer to the Promised Land, the beloved community of God."

Shane Claiborne, author, activist and recovering sinner

"*Welcoming Justice* represents the perfect marriage of social justice and schol-
arly reflection. Far too often, those endeavors are not connected, leaving
either effort impoverished. Everyone interested in thoughtful and just social
change will find this book richly rewarding."

Dr. Susan M. Glisson, executive director, The William Winter Institute for
Racial Reconciliation, University of Mississippi

"The blood that runs through the veins of our nation is a muddy river; its
waters are deep with honor and shame, joy and pain, compassion and exploitation. Charles Marsh and John Perkins are incredible navigators in the
murky waters of race and reconciliation. To see the past, present and future
of 'the dream' of the beloved community through the eyes of Perkins and
Marsh is to see a resurrection of hope. These are two men who live out the
ideas they speak about with eloquence and beauty. If words are the scaffold-·
ing we build our lives on, this book lays a true and elegant foundation."

Jon Foreman, songwriter, musician and cofounder of the alternative rock bands
Switchfoot and Fiction Family

"Growing up in a Korean American immigrant church context, I did not hear the name John Perkins all that often. Since those early years, I have made a concerted effort to learn as much as possible about the work of one of the most important American Christian voices of the twentieth and twenty-first centuries. This book provides important insights into the life, testimony, theology and ministry of John Perkins. It is both a work of inspiration and a work of history (reflecting the leanings of the dual authors) that must be read by any student or practitioner of social justice ministry. The book provides novices, faithful servants and even the weary laborers the inspiration to persevere in God's kingdom work. John Perkins and Charles Marsh provide for us a view of compassion, mercy and justice ministry that needs to be heeded in the context of a new evangelicalism in North America."

Soong-Chan Rah, Milton B. Engebretson Associate Professor of Church Growth and Evangelism, North Park Theological Seminary, and author of *The Next Evangelicalism*

"For years, John Perkins and Charles Marsh have been two of our most important figures in the discussion and pursuit of reconciliation. Now, from their passion for justice, their love of the gospel, and their friendship with one another, comes this gem, which may be the most important book either of them has written yet."

Lauren F. Winner, author of *Girl Meets God*

WELCOMING
JUSTICE

God's Movement
Toward Beloved Community

CHARLES MARSH
& JOHN M. PERKINS

Foreword by PHILIP YANCEY

Resources for Reconciliation

series editors

EMMANUEL KATONGOLE & CHRIS RICE

IVP Books

An imprint of InterVarsity Press
Downers Grove, Illinois

InterVarsity Press
P.O. Box 1400, Downers Grove, IL 60515-1426
World Wide Web: www.ivpress.com
E-mail: email@ivpress.com

InterVarsity Press® is the book-publishing division of InterVarsity Christian Fellowship/USA®, a movement of students and faculty active on campus at hundreds of universities, colleges and schools of nursing in the United States of America, and a member movement of the International Fellowship of Evangelical Students. For information about local and regional activities, write Public Relations Dept., InterVarsity Christian Fellowship/USA, 6400 Schroeder Rd., P.O. Box 7895, Madison, WI 53707-7895, or visit the IVCF website at <www.intervarsity.org>.

All Scripture quotations, unless otherwise indicated, are taken from the Holy Bible, Today's New International Version™ Copyright © 2001 by International Bible Society. All rights reserved.

Design: Rebecca Larson
Images: Ascension by Rick Beerhorst/Eyekons <www.eyekons.com>
Author photo: Kendall Cox

ISBN 978-0-8308-3453-2

Printed in the United States of America ∞

Library of Congress Cataloging-in-Publication Data

Marsh, Charles, 1958-
  Welcoming justice: God's movement toward beloved community /
  Charles Marsh and John M. Perkins.
     p. cm.——(Resources for reconciliation)
  Includes bibliographical references.
  ISBN 978-0-8308-3453-2 (pbk.: alk. paper)
  1. Christianity and justice. 2. Civil rights——Religious
  aspects——Christianity. 3. United States——Race relations. 4.
  Minorities——Civil rights——United States——History——20th century. I.
  Perkins, John, 1930- II. Title.
  BR115.J8M38 2009
  261.8——dc22
                    2009026596

P	21	20	19	18	17	16	15	14	13	12	11	10	9	8	7	6	5
Y	30	29	28	27	26	25	24	23	22	21	20	19	18	17	16		

Contents

Series Preface

$\mathcal{A}$ partnership between InterVarsity Press and the Center for Reconciliation at Duke Divinity School, Resources for Reconciliation books address what it means to pursue hope in areas of brokenness, including the family, the city, the poor, the disabled, Christianity and Islam, racial and ethnic divisions, violent conflicts, and the environment. The series seeks to offer a fresh and distinctive vision for reconciliation as God's mission and a journey toward God's new creation in Christ. Each book is authored by two leading voices, one in the field of practice or grassroots experience, the other from the academy. Each book is grounded in the biblical story, engages stories and places of pain and hope, and seeks to help readers to live faithfully—a rich mix of theology, context and practice.

This book series was born out of the mission of the Duke Divinity School Center for Reconciliation: *Advancing God's mission of reconciliation in a divided world by cultivating new leaders, communicating wisdom and hope, and connecting in outreach to strengthen leadership.* A divided world needs people with the vision, spiritual maturity and daily skills integral to the journey of reconciliation. The church needs fresh resources—a mix of biblical vision, social skills of social and historical analysis, and practical gifts of spirituality and social leadership—in order to pursue reconciliation in real places, from congregations to communities.

The ministry of reconciliation is not reserved for experts. It is the core of God's mission and an everyday call of the Christian life. These books are written to equip and stimulate God's people to be more faithful ambassadors of reconciliation in a fractured world.

For more information, email the Duke Divinity School Center for Reconciliation at reconciliation@div.duke.edu, or visit our website: <www.dukereconciliation.com>.

Emmanuel Katongole
Chris Rice
Center codirectors and series editors

Foreword

$\mathcal{O}$n November 4, 2008, I boarded a plane for Memphis just before polling places closed in the east. Stepping off the plane three hours later, I turned to the first person I saw, an African American baggage handler. "Do you know who won the election?" He proceeded to give me a complete breakdown of the Electoral College results and which states Barack Obama would need to clinch victory. I got a strong clue as to how much this election meant to a people who have spent far more years oppressed than liberated by democracy.

The next day I toured the National Civil Rights Museum built around the motel where Martin Luther King Jr. was assassinated. For several hours I revisited the scenes I had known so well as a teenager coming of age in the South. The brave college students in Greensboro, North Carolina, who sat at a lunch counter as goons stamped out cigarettes in their hair, squirted mustard and ketchup in their faces, then knocked them off the stools and kicked them while white policemen looked on, laughing. The eerie scenes of weightless children flying through mist in Birmingham, Alabama, propelled by high-powered fire hoses. The Freedom Ride bus burned in Alabama, the corpses unburied in Mississippi.

Looking back, it seems incredible to imagine such ferocity directed against people who were seeking the basic ingredients of human dignity: the right to vote, to eat in restaurants and stay in motels, to attend college (two hundred National Guardsmen escorted James Meredith to his first class at the University of Mississippi, and even so people died in the ensuing riots).

Outside the museum, words from King's final "I have been to the mountaintop" speech are forged in steel, words that caught in my throat on a sunny day mere hours after Obama was elected as our first African American president: "I may not get there with you, but I want you to know that we, as a people, will get to the Promised Land." The next day King died in a pool of blood on the very spot where I was standing.

Although many Christians have important policy differences with President Obama, this historical moment offers a golden time for reflection and, yes, repentance over our share in the sin of racism that has marked this nation since its founding. It took Southern Baptists 150 years to apologize for their support of slavery, and not until 2008 did Bob Jones University admit their error in barring black students before 1971. Their words of apology—"We failed to accurately represent the Lord and to fulfill the commandment to love others as ourselves"—apply to many of us, for many conservative Christians vigorously opposed the movement. Can we now respond to a leader's call for healing and reconciliation?

* * *

I have much in common with Charles Marsh, a Southern Baptist minister's son growing up in a small southern town in the late sixties who began to question the assumptions of his family and the surrounding racist culture. I have followed with great interest his writings on the topic, such as *God's Long Summer: Stories of Faith and Civil Rights* and *The Last Days: A Son's Story of Sin and Segregation at the Dawn of a New South*.

And John Perkins played a key role in my own enlightenment on racial issues. In 1974, ten years after the landmark Civil Rights Bill, I accepted his invitation to visit the small town of Mendenhall, just south of Jackson. As a black minister, Perkins had lived through the worst nightmares of the Civil Rights movement. I heard the stories of his own encounters with violent sheriffs and the Ku Klux Klan during the week I spent in Mississippi. I slept on a foldout sofa in the living room of his home, which meant I got very little sleep since Perkins went to bed late and rose long before sunrise to read his Bible and pore over newspapers and journals piled on his kitchen table. I doubt I was the first white guest to integrate Perkins's home, though he had been the first black guest in many white homes during his speaking tours across the country. We had much time to talk, and I learned to appreciate Perkins's graciousness in reaching out to the white community from whom he had received such abuse.

Most local ministers of Perkins's evangelical persuasion stuck to preaching the gospel and left human needs to social workers and government agencies. Perkins accepted the broader mission proclaimed by Jesus:

- to preach the gospel to the poor
- to heal the brokenhearted
- to proclaim liberty to the captives
- and recovery of sight to the blind
- to set at liberty those who are oppressed
- to proclaim the acceptable year of the Lord

After one horrific night of torture in jail, Perkins underwent a crisis of faith. "It was time for me to decide if I really did believe what I'd so often professed, that only in the love of Christ, not in power of violence, is there any hope for me or the world. I began to see how hate could destroy me. In the end, I had to agree with Dr. King that God wanted us to return good for evil, not evil for evil. 'Love your enemy,' Jesus said. And I determined to do it. It's a profound, mysterious truth, Jesus' concept of love overpowering hate. I may not see it in my lifetime. But I know it's true. Because on that bed, full of bruises and stitches, God made it true in me. I got a transfusion of hope."

Over the next decades, Perkins moved to Los Angeles, where he founded both a local and national organization for community development based on what he had learned in Mendenhall, then returned to Mississippi to lead a movement for racial reconciliation. John Perkins's son Spencer soon took up the torch, joining with Chris Rice, a young white man, to write and speak on the topic of racial reconciliation. Tragically, Spencer died of heart failure at the age of forty-three.

In some ways, *Welcoming Justice* recapitulates the message proclaimed first by the father and then the son. John Perkins, an elderly African American who has become a kind of guru on the topic of race and hands-on community development, joins with Charles Marsh, a white scholar who directs the Project on Lived Theology at the University of Virginia. Both are committed to the belief that the church can play a central role in racial healing. As Marsh writes, "It is unlikely that anyone has ever read Nietzsche's *The Antichrist* or Derrida's *Dissemination* and been inspired to open a soup kitchen. . . . Still, my research has shown me that only as long as the Civil Rights movement remained anchored in the church—in the energies, convictions and images of the biblical narrative and the worshiping community—did the movement have a vision."

Martin Luther King Jr. used to say that the real goal was not to defeat the white man but "to awaken a sense of shame within the oppressor and challenge his false sense of superiority. . . . The end is reconciliation; the end is redemption; the end is the creation of the beloved community." Sadly, that exalted vision got lost in the Black Power movement and in the racial divide that seemed to widen socially even as legal barriers fell. Together, Perkins and Marsh are attempting to restore the vision, both conceptually and practically, showing how theology can indeed be lived out in a multicultural society despite its deeply stained past. I know of no better time to attempt such a project, and no team better equipped to accomplish it.

Philip Yancey

I

The Unfinished Business of the Civil Rights Movement

CHARLES MARSH

When Martin Luther King Jr. moved to Montgomery, Alabama, in the spring of 1954, civil rights activism was not on his mind. King went to Montgomery because the Dexter Avenue Baptist Church offered a great salary, a comfortable parsonage and a highly educated congregation. The fact that King wasn't looking to become an activist did not come as a disappointment to the congregation. Dexter Avenue had no interest in hiring a racial crusader. Its members had long prided themselves on their access to white elites and their own relative social privilege. Though they shared a common hope for a future without Jim Crow, they were not going to ignite the fires of dissent.

The day after Rosa Parks refused to move from her seat in the front of the bus, Ralph Abernathy talked King into accepting the leadership of the Montgomery Improvement Association (MIA). But King accepted only after being reassured that the boycott would be over in a day. As president of the MIA, King made clear in his first list of demands, which were presented to National City Buslines, that the protest was *not* about challenging segregation. The NAACP found his demands so weak that they refused to endorse his list.

At that time, King was no fan of nonviolence either. Glenn Smiley, a white staff member visiting Montgomery with the Fellowship of Reconciliation, claimed to have discovered "an arsenal" in his parsonage.[1] "When I was in graduate school," King had said, "I thought the only way we could solve our problem . . . was an armed revolt."[2]

By the end of the second month of the boycott, King had fallen into despair about his leadership and the direction of the boycott. On a gloomy day in January 1956, fearing that he was a complete failure, King offered his resignation as the president of the MIA. It was not accepted, but King's doubts about his own abilities as a pastor and organizer remained real and unabated.

Later in that month, King returned home to his parsonage around midnight after a long day of organizational meetings. His wife and young daughter were already in bed, and King was eager to join them. But a threatening call—the kind of call he was getting as many as thirty to forty times a day—interrupted his attempt to get some much-needed rest. When he tried to go back to bed, for some reason he could not shake the menacing voice that kept repeating the hateful words in his head.

King got up, made a pot of coffee and sat down at his kitchen table. With his head buried in his hands, he cried out to God. There in his kitchen in the middle of the night, when he had by his own account come to the end of his strength, King met the living Christ in an experience that would carry him through the remainder of his life. "I heard the voice of Jesus saying still to fight on," King later recalled. "He promised never to leave me, never to leave me alone. No never alone. No never alone. He promised never to leave me, no never alone."[3]

In the stillness of the Alabama night, the voice of Jesus proved more convincing than the threatening voice of the anonymous caller. The voice of Jesus gave him the courage to press through the tumultuous year of 1956 to the victorious end of the Montgomery Bus Boycott. More than that, it gave him a vision for ministry that would drive him for the rest of his life.

When the MIA held a weeklong Institute on Nonviolence and Social Change near the end of their boycott, King looked back at their long hard struggle for justice and made clear its ultimate aim. Though a boycott had been necessary to end discrimination in Montgomery, that boycott was not the end. "The end," King said, "is reconciliation, the end is redemption, the end is the creation of the beloved community."[4]

I begin with this remarkable moment from the early days of King's involvement in the Civil Rights movement because it points us toward the unfinished business of welcoming justice, the theme of this book. King shows us the plot line of the Civil

Rights movement. More than that, he points to the very goal of God's movement in the world. God gathers us into the family of faith not only for our own sake, but also so that we might welcome justice and build beloved communities for the sake of the world. That is the purpose that drives followers of the risen Christ. It is the movement of the Spirit that began at Pentecost and has continued in faithful communities of discipleship throughout every generation. It is the theological vision that we need desperately to reclaim in our time.

A UNIFYING THEOLOGICAL VISION

For more than ten years now, I have been writing and researching "lived theology," exploring the way our ideas about God shape our moral convictions and ideas about community, justice and racial reconciliation. This has not been merely an academic exercise for me.

I grew up in the South in the 1960s. In 1967 my family moved from a sleepy town in south Alabama to Laurel, Mississippi, which had earned the reputation as the epicenter of southern terrorism, home to the White Knights of the Ku Klux Klan and their daily installments of misery and violence. My father was a big-hearted son of the Son with his eyes set on denominational prestige, a young preacher at First Baptist Church and cheerfully indifferent to the racial turmoil he was moving his family right into the middle of. The Civil Rights movement, which I observed from various stages of pubescent awkwardness, was our trial by fire.

My dad's embrace of the reconciling energies of the faith was at first slow and hesitant, though finally it was undeniable. To his congregation of Citizens Councilors and segregationists, he called into question the church's "closed-door policy" and eventually preached the sermon "Amazing Grace for Every Race."

In graduate school in the 1980s I was trained in philosophical theology and modern Christian thought. In the early 1990s I found myself teaching at a Jesuit college in Baltimore, writing academic monographs and being about all those things you need to do to get tenure. After finishing a book in 1994 on German theologian and Christian martyr Dietrich Bonhoeffer, I was surprised to discover that my thoughts and dreams, and increasingly my journals and notebooks, were filled with memories of my childhood in the Deep South. I had planned to write a book on the doctrine of the Trinity but was having trouble concentrating on this marvelous sacred mystery.

Though my childhood had been very intense and eventful, the South had changed. I had not thought a whole lot about those years while I was in college or graduate school, but now I could think of nothing else. I became suddenly haunted by the memories of those years. Long forgotten fears became once again vivid and alive; memories burst into consciousness like floodwaters.

So in the summer of 1994—thirty years after Freedom Summer of 1964, when students went to the South to help with voter registration for disenfranchised African Americans—I got in my Honda wagon one morning and headed south, with not much more than a full tank of gas, a microcassette recorder and a credit card. This veering off of the straight and narrow road of my academic training changed my life, and it gently invited me into a different kind of theological education.

I was taught to listen more closely to voices outside the academic guild, to engage the subject with humility but also with courage, to be charitable but not to use a false sense of charity as an excuse for risking the concrete word. I learned that theology needs a place.

The experience also brought home to me, in a particularly intense way, the questions Why am I a scholar? and Who am I serving? "You gotta serve somebody, right?" St. Bob sang. Only my professional colleagues? Or a wider audience of men and women who seek the flourishing of human community, who seek justice and practice mercy, who serve the poor?

Once in an interview, a kindly minister who had been recalling his years as a staff member of the National Council of Churches and his role in the 1965 March on Selma, paused and said, "You know, your generation is a bunch of wimps." The least I could do—being a wimp and all—was to ask a few hard questions about my own vocation as a scholar and teacher and somehow try to make the connection back to life.

I was able to see too how the Civil Rights movement that took place in the 1950s and 1960s not only changed unjust laws but also brought about a spiritual awakening, and I am further convinced that this story teaches us even today important lessons about what Dr. Perkins called a holistic faith, about the renewal of the church's mission to take part in the healing of our broken and violent and blistered world. The Civil Rights movement teaches us that faith is authentic when it stays close to the ground. And it reminds us of faith's essential affirmations: showing hospitality to strangers and outcasts; affirming the dignity of created life; reclaiming the ideals of love, honesty and truth; embracing the preferential option of nonviolence; and practicing justice and mercy.

Until 1964 the Civil Rights movement in the South was unified and sustained by a vision of "beloved community." King's speech at the end of the Montgomery Bus Boycott offers us a key to understanding what the spirit of the movement was about. For many people, the movement moved on, served its basic purposes or collapsed in chaos. But for those who understand civil rights to be part of God's larger movement in the world, the movement continues. This book is about the movement that started with Abraham, captivated America's attention for a moment in the 1950s and 1960s and still goes on today in countless forgotten places on the margins of our society. It's about the God movement that is embodied in the lives of John and Vera Mae Perkins.

I am delighted to have the opportunity to write this book with John Perkins. In so many ways, he embodies the best of what I have learned about a theology that participates in God's peaceable movement in the world. Stories of people like John and Vera Mae offer a wonderful and altogether persuasive response to those who say that Christianity is irrelevant or even harmful to society. We see in their richly lived theology that authentic faith not only heightens our perception of the world; it also provides the resources, the disciplines and the gifts we need to keep our hands to the plow.

My secularist colleagues in the academy are not very convincing on the question of why we ought to love the broken and the outcast and build beloved community. It is all well and good for the brilliant and often helpful theorist Anthony Appiah to advise us to "live with fractured identities; engage in identity's play . . . recognize contingency, and above all practice irony."[5] But what might it mean to settle down after "identity's play" has run its course and build community among the hopeless and excluded in places where irony is a condescending shrug?

It is unlikely that anyone has ever read Nietzsche's *The Antichrist* or Derrida's *Dissemination* and been inspired to open a soup kitchen. It would be wonderful if one did, because the work of justice and mercy needs the energies and talents of compassionate people, believer(s) or not. The Christian should welcome all men and women to kingdom work with a gracious and open heart. And, of course, many people who are not Christians have dedicated time and energy to the pursuit of social justice, from working in soup kitchens to marching for peace—and who knows, maybe even some Nietzscheans and deconstructionists have as well.

Still, my research has shown me that only as long as the Civil Rights movement remained anchored in the church—in the energies, convictions and images of the biblical narrative and the worshiping community—did the movement have a vision. The work of organizing and building communities in distressed and excluded places was about celebrating the common grace of women and men, black and white, the privileged and the poor, who found themselves together, miraculously, in the South, working in common cause for a more just and human social order. To the extent that the Civil Rights movement lost this vision, it lost its way. But where the vision was sustained—in the hundreds of Christian community development ministries inspired by John and Vera Mae Perkins, among other often overlooked places—God's movement was nourished and flourishes still. Though frequently forgotten by historians and policymakers, God's movement is the most powerful source of social change in our society.

When you listen to movement veterans tell their stories, you often hear testimonials that have their home in the church. So, as I see it, what's lost when you strip away the religious conviction is appreciation of those very sources that energize and sustain compassion—and that continue to inspire redemptive action in the world.

Visit a hospitality house, a tutorial program for low-income children, an AIDS clinic, a hunger relief agency, a Habitat for Humanity site, an administrative building where a student group is sitting in support of a living wage for university workers—you will find there people who are moved to act for others, who live passionately into the depths and breadth of the world's concrete needs because they see a light shining in the darkness; who believe that transcendence empowers rather than diminishes the love of life, that hope and miracle and mystery animate the protest against cruelty, focus moral energies and heighten discernment of those places in the world that call out for healing and wholeness. The philosopher Søren Kierkegaard wrote of faith as the most complex artwork, and yet the most exquisite. And indeed, if you listen closely, you will hear that the men and women who work day in and day out in inauspicious places to bring healing to our broken and blistered world are people who are carried and strengthened and nourished by deep spiritual waters, who show that vivid realism about the human condition is more honest and clearly drawn against horizons of grace.

THE ROOTS OF OUR PRESENT PROBLEM

A little history can help us understand the gifts that John Perkins offers the church today. In late 1964, despite an impressive slate of civil rights legislation, the vision of beloved community began to fragment in ways that continue to shape and frustrate racial peace in America. The reasons for this fragmentation are complex, disputed and hard to sort out. By the end of that decisive year, though, the Student Nonviolent Coordinating Committee (SNCC) had clearly moved away from Christian formulations of nonviolence and beloved community. The "circle of trust" began to forget its lineage as a child of the church. Some members even sought to obliterate this identity.

"We should never again seek to involve the church in actions of SNCC," Stanley Wise would say in a staff meeting in 1966.[6] The goal of redeemed society, it was duly noted, remained only the minority position of John Lewis, Charles Sherrod and a few other believers who lacked credibility among the new SNCC vanguard. What had begun with Fannie Lou Hamer's exuberant affirmation, "I've got the light of freedom," concluded with one young activist's arrogant claim that Ms. Hamer was "no longer relevant," no longer at "our level of development." "We have closed ourselves in a haven and the movement has passed us by," a dejected staff member said.[7]

Without a spiritual vision, there would be no more summer projects, no more coalitions between local organizers and the white campuses, no more innovations in community action. SNCC began to divide the world between the forces of light and the forces of darkness, and its Manichean perspective brought about a perception in the changing youth movement of the United States as malevolent and beyond redemption. America was ontologically evil. Whiteness was ontologically evil. Most importantly, concrete social reform was not possible.

Removed from its home in the church, the work of building beloved community withered and died. Unanchored from its animating vision of beloved community, the Civil Rights movement lost its spiritual and moral focus. At the same time, it also became confused about organizing strategies. This is a little understood but important point.

Without its unifying spiritual vision, the movement's goal was no longer to identify particular social and economic ills that could be improved upon through political organizing and social reform. The new goals were rather more elusive: "End racism"; "Change [the] system"; "Develop [the] concept of humanism." These goals indicated a striking change from the days when voter registration, political organizing and educational reform were the measure of success. The movement went cosmic, but cosmic ambitions dis-connected from local commitments created strategic confusions.

On the eve of the new decade of the 1970s, one journalist wrote: "In America of the late 1960s, with its congested cities and streets, its high crime rates, its guns and knives, its instant communications that pipe reports of civil disturbances into ev-ery household, its divisions and strife, its overbearing technol-ogy, its mass culture, mass education, and mass government, history seems to cry out for a new tradition that would provide a nonviolent means for change and for expression and protest."

This was the observation of New York Times reporter John Her-bers in his essential book, The Lost Priority: What Happened to the Civil Rights Movement in America? Herbers continued, "Martin Lu-ther King and his nonviolent armies seemed for a time to have implanted this kind of tradition. Anyone who followed the civil rights movement could not escape the feeling that here was a spirit that could enlighten the country. In those days they talked of saving not only themselves but the soul of America as well, and after some of the great movements they would talk about saving the world with nonviolence. But nonviolence as a national and mystical movement . . . died."[8]

Other banners flew in the chaotic winds. For a few humorless children of the movement, the emerging culture of sensitivity training illuminated the zones of white redemption. Absolution had never been so easy: a few hours in a seminar room and a dec-laration of white depravity was a small price to pay for centuries of slavery and genocide. Not only was the new race therapy a lot easier than organizing in poor communities; it also presupposed the utter naiveté of King's vision and quietly mocked the search for beloved community as the illusion of unanalyzed souls, which had been racist to the core all along.

No one was quite sure where to go from here. Black militants were tired of King's theology of nonviolence. Conservatives had not yet learned to turn the Civil Rights legacy to their political advantage—to replay King's reference to "the content of our character" as a call to politically disengaged pietism. White liberals were feeling betrayal. King's dissent on their war in Vietnam left them aghast at his ingratitude.[9]

In his 1967 address "A Time to Break Silence," at Riverside Church in New York City, King reaffirmed his "commitment to the ministry of Jesus Christ" and proceeded to preach the hard message that the Christian's basic obligation is obedience "to the one who loved his enemies so fully that he died for them."[10] The soul of America could never be redeemed so long as it trusted the god of its own violent ambitions. "The War in Vietnam is but a symptom of a far deeper malady within the American spirit," he prophesied. Although many Americans had stopped listening, King resolved that America's only hope lay in repentance—in a repentance that took the form of willingness to be a servant nation to the poor of the earth. Sadly, King would not live to say much more.

HOPE FOR OUR TIME

More than forty years after King's assassination, his theological vision of redemption, reconciliation and the creation of beloved community has never been more important. Especially at a time when the language of faith is so often trivialized and politicized in the public square, we need people who help us see what an enfleshed church looks like. This is why the life and witness of John and Vera Mae Perkins are so important.

In February of 1970, John Perkins was beaten nearly to death by police officers in the town of Brandon, Mississippi. While recovering from injuries in a hospital in the black hamlet of Mound Bayou, he received a vision of Jesus suffering on the cross. Perkins emerged from six months of treatment at Tuft Medical Center with a new conviction that Christian love could not rest content until it found space for the neighbor and the enemy. He would make his life a parable of forgiveness and reconciliation: "I might go so far as to say that I experienced a second conversion while I lay in that hospital bed. It was a conversion of love and forgiveness."[11]

Perkins began thinking about the unfinished business of the Civil Rights movement. In his talks and seminars, he made frequent mention of "three Rs" of community building: relocation, redistribution and reconciliation. These comprised the trinity of disciplines that became the core of his expanded ministry. While partly descriptive of his work in Mendenhall since 1964, the three Rs also illuminated a way for Christians in forgotten places to go about the unfinished business of the Civil Rights movement.

Relocation. Relocation means incarnational evangelism, the lived expression of the great christological theme that Jesus Chrsit "did not consider equality with God something to be grasped" but took on "the very nature of a servant" (Philippians

2). Perkins showed that the activist and organizer will only cease to patronize the poor when they live in community with them and approach them in a spirit of compassion and with the willingness to serve. "Living involvement," Perkins said, "turns poor people from statistics into our friends."[12]

Redistribution. Redistribution means sharing talents and resources with the poor, but it also means observable changes in public policy and voting habits. Public policy would need to be accompanied by a Christ-shaped willingness to offer one's skills and knowledge as gifts to others. Indeed—quite apart from specific policty recommendations—Perkins imagined the Christian community as a distinctive social order that models the redistribution of wealth in demanding and faithful ways.[13]

Perkins explained, "[There] are heavy social implications to the equality expressed in God's spiritual activity in creation. Perhaps the heaviest is Christ's identification with the poor. . . . He calls the poor person his brother: 'Whatever you did for the humblest of my brothers you did for me' (Matt. 25:40). *God meant for equality to be expressed in terms of economics.*"[14] The Fall of Adam and Eve resulted in the "pollution and distortion of the equality which he intended," which is seen nowhere more tragically than in economic brokenness. For this reason, the body of Christ must be marked as an alternative social order that "breaks the cycle of wealth and poverty."[15]

Reconciliation. Reconciliation means embodying the message that "ye are all one in Christ Jesus" and that Christ has "destroyed the barrier, the dividing wall of hostility" in lived social experience. The visible demonstration of "a brotherhood of intertwined lives"—even if it was just white and black folk hanging out in the inauspicious community center at Perkins's Voice of Calvary ministry—subverted the godforsaken spaces of racial segregation unlike any individual act of racial heroism. The hard work of reconciliation is a different matter indeed than emotion catharsis or psychological affirmation. Reconciliation may produce handshakes and hugs and the tears of reunion, but without confrontation and corrective action it is empty, Perkins said.[16]

With his three Rs and his incredible energy, Perkins charted a new course for building beloved community in America—one that defied conventional political categories. Leadership must be based in poor communities and eventually rise out of these communities, Perkins insisted, but at the same time, outsiders would be invited to play a critical role in fostering indigenous leadership. In Perkins's view, civil rights organizations such as SNCC and Congress of Racial Equality (CORE) too often racialized and politicized the role of the outsider at the expense of people in poor communities. Patronization is a worry only when outsiders fail to discern the gifts of the poor—their loyalty, fragility, creativity and holiness—and deny the importance of black leadership. When this happens, outsiders are quick to impose their own plans on the poor and slow to see the wisdom in the local story.

Without backing away from his support of integration, equal opportunity, affirmative action and welfare, Perkins further concluded that government programs alone failed to address the deeper sources of hopelessness in black communities. The Civil

Rights movement focused its energies on protesting legal injustice and bringing an end to the reign of white terror—for this was what the times required. But despite its glorious accomplishments, the Civil Rights movement failed to offer a compelling account of the spiritual energies and disciplines required to sustain beloved community. And as a result, so many of its leaders failed to give detail and depth to a holistic gospel. Perkins's witness helps us see how most of the Civil Rights movement failed to reckon with the truth that discipleship to Jesus Christ is the most enduring source of renewed social practices, care for the poor, costly forgiveness and reparations for slavery.

Christian hope in our time demands that we reckon with this truth.

PROPHET TO THE CHURCH

After 1970, John Perkins began using the term *prophetic* to describe the countercultural practices of the Christian community. He thought hard about the connection between racism in the South and national military spending, nuclear stockpiling, and the political neglect of the poor. And he questioned America as his friend Fannie Lou Hamer had done in her haunting testimony at the 1964 National Democratic Convention: "Is *this* America, the land of the free and the home of the brave?"[17] "We have so organized and incorporated the church into our economic system," Perkins said, "that not only can't that system be disciplined, but if one does speak against it he or she is speaking against God and America and must be locked up."[18]

An evangelical Bible teacher, Perkins moved away from the old fundamentalist preoccupation with the fate of the individual soul and began asking questions of a directly social intent: "What is God's program on earth and how do I fit in?"[19] This is essentially the question of the kingdom. To be a public disciple means finding a place in the world where the kingdom of God is taking shape and getting yourself there.[20]

Yet Perkins's new message was not a simple shift to the social gospel or liberation theology. An evangelical emphasis on personal relationship with Jesus remained at the center of his social vision. Perkins's point was that individual transformation required a disciplined and impassioned commitment to the healing of the social order. In the creation of the world, God fashioned man and woman with the basic needs for food, shelter, clothing, clean air and health. These needs signal a "certain haunting equality," he said in his classic work *A Quiet Revolution*—a bottom-line description of human dignity which shapes the Christian's entire outlook on social existence and political community.

Though many conservative supporters of Perkins's ministry would praise his candid assessment of welfare's disincentives to work, he made clear as early as the mid-seventies that the gospel involved "redemptive release" from all forms of physical and economic oppression, and that Jesus Christ identified with the poor "to the point of equating himself with the poor person."[21] The presumption throughout Perkins's theology of community is that a people transformed and mobilized by Jesus Christ in their institutional behavior will consistently support economic policies preferential to the poor, not out of obligation to law but as an expression of public discipleship. John Perkins might be considered the father of the faith-based movement, but the faith-based movement in its historical origins was about reading the Bible as the comprehensive divine plan of human liberation with resources for countercultural action and community building.

Perkins's theses add up to a social agenda more radical than any advanced by the Civil Rights movement. In Perkins's three Rs we find a trinity of disciplines that illuminates the areas where the Civil Rights movement failed to deliver on its most basic promises: solidarity with the poor, minority economic power and racial reconciliation.

Over and above all movements for social justice is God's movement, "cutting through all these movements as their hidden sense and motor, the movement of God's history," the creative origin of any movement toward human liberation and solidarity.[22] Martin Luther King Jr. spoke of the "spiritual movement in Montgomery," Fannie Lou Hamer of the "New Kingdom in Mississippi." These are the historical antecedents and theological cousins of what Perkins calls the "quiet revolution."

This movement that Perkins has both inspired and embodied helps us see the hidden theological meaning of the search for beloved community. What is that hidden meaning? Perkins says, "God made His love visible to the world in the person of Jesus Christ. And Jesus Christ made His love visible to the world in His unselfish death on the cross for our sins. So it becomes our responsibility as the Body of Christ to so live out His life on earth as to make the love of God visible in our time. And in our community."[23]

Against the political and cultural captivity of American Christendom, Perkins claims that nothing less than the credibility of the gospel is at stake. Discipleship to Jesus Christ requires us to reevaluate our political preferences, personal desires, prejudices, opinions and economic policies in the light of God's moral demands. Christians in North America must be known as people with a burden for the poor and oppressed, who "plead the case of the poor, defending the weak, helping the helpless. . . . We must as Christians seek justice by coming up with means of redistributing goods and wealth to those in need."[24]

Let me conclude this chapter with a theological affirmation: The habits and practices that sustain beloved community are the gifts of the church. Broken and fallible, the church is nevertheless the one enduring source of forgiveness and reconciliation in our violent world. "The church," Perkins has said, "is the only institution I know of that offers the basis for a discipline, a commitment, a hope, a truth that is stronger than racism and stronger than any institutional form that clothes racism."[25] Perkins's witness offers a powerful source of hope for the church that is also great hope for the world. To join with him in the unfinished business of the Civil Rights movement is to give ourselves body and soul to God's movement in the world today.

2

The Cultural Captivity of the Church

JOHN M. PERKINS

*I*n 1960, God called Vera Mae and me back to the place where we'd grown up in Mendenhall, Mississippi. We started telling Bible stories to kids in the public schools, and I thought that's what I was going to do for the rest of my life. The work was so rewarding. But in the early 1960s, poverty in Mississippi became a national issue. Segregated education had conditioned us to think that white is right and black is bad, but the psychologist Kenneth Clark had proved in the *Brown v. Board of Education* case that separate was not only unequal, it was also harmful to black people. In the Mississippi Delta we were suffering from that kind of unequal education in the early 1960s, so President Kennedy set up Head Start programs for nutrition and education. The whole country started to pay attention to poverty in Mississippi.

About that time, I met a white pastor in Mendenhall. I liked this guy, and I started to realize that he liked me. He was a theologically educated man, and I think he was impressed that a black man could understand the basic tenets of the faith as I did. Somehow, we became friends. I knew I needed his help and he respected me, so we started to meet and talk about how we could work together.

I told this white pastor what I perceived the problem in our community to be: I saw the best people leaving the community when they graduated from high school. They were leaving for New York and Chicago, and they weren't coming back. Anyone who got an education couldn't see how it was relevant to their community and its development. If we were going to make a difference in Mississippi, we were going to have to help poor kids get an education and then come back home. We had to show them that their communities were important because God said they were important. I shared this vision for ministry with my white friend, and he said he wanted to help me. This was in rural Mississippi in 1965.

Like any good pastor, my friend decided that he needed to teach these ideas to his congregation before he led them into a new ministry. I imagine he talked to them about the importance of missions and started inviting them to think about what that could look like in Mendenhall. But his church was threatened by the idea of working with a black minister. They were as shocked as I was that a white minister wanted to work with me, and they rejected my friend. He couldn't handle their rejection, so he killed himself.

That's when I started to realize that the church had become captive to our culture. We'd taken the good news of God's love that's supposed to burn through racial and social divisions and turned it into a religion that reinforced the status quo. That's the Christianity we've inherited in this country, and that's what our missionaries have gone around the world preaching. We've over-evangelized the world too lightly, and the church has reinforced America's problems more than we've given people reason to believe in something new. I started to see that in a little town in Mississippi forty years ago, and I've spent the rest of my life trying to preach a gospel that burns through racial and cultural barriers and reconciles people to God and one another.

In 1960 I thought God had called me to tell Bible stories to school kids. I would have been more than happy to do that work for the rest of my life. But my white friend's suicide showed me that I was called to preach the good news of Jesus Christ to white people. Looking back, I guess that was a unique call for a third-grade drop-out from rural Mississippi. There aren't many black preachers who are called to evangelize white people, but that's what I've spent a large portion of my life doing. I think it's because my friend who killed himself showed me how racism holds white people captive.

During the sixties, when I started my ministry, we were angry about racism and injustice. We sang "Do Right, White Man" and confronted white power. Stokely Carmichael and Malcolm X convinced many of us that Black Power was our only hope.

Most black folks saw white people as mean and wicked. But I knew they were broken and lost. They needed to hear the truth that would set them free.

Reacting against white imperialistic theology, the Civil Rights movement developed a philosophy in which race trumped the gospel. Of course, the movement came out of the churches, and its greatest power always came from the Christian faith. It's a miracle that the faith was not destroyed throughout the years of witnessing white folks use a theology based on the same God to further oppress us black folks.

THE SHARED WOUNDS OF OPPRESSION

Our poor black communities cannot hide the effect that racism and oppression have had on us. We suffer from broken families, broken communities and a broken church. All you have to do to see this is to come to my neighborhood in West Jackson, Mississippi. So many of our young black men have bought into this "jailhouse" culture, and you can see them on the streets with their pants hanging down and their underwear showing. Now, there was a time when that was a statement of rebellion against the racism of this country's prison system. They don't let you have belts in prison, you know. And they don't worry too much about giving you the right size pants either. So somebody somewhere decided he would show society what he thought by dropping his pants in their face. There was a time when that act of revolt had meaning. But it's become a style. Our young people don't know why they wear their pants like that. They just do.

Our poor, young men don't know why they're angry. They just are. Kids in our neighborhood have lived such a segregated life that they don't know any white people to be mad at. But they have internalized this rebellious anger, and it has turned into an unrecognized self-hatred. They kill the people they love most because they don't know what to do with the fact that they've been taught to hate themselves. Meanwhile, the church does little to tell them who they really are. We haven't taught them a language of affirmation.

When I was a young man, the Civil Rights movement had to tell us "black is beautiful." We started wearing Afros to say that black hair was just as good as white hair, and we grew beards to insist that we were men, not boys. I still wear a goatee, and I don't plan to shave it. But for me the whole "black is beautiful" movement exposed the depth of the damage we had suffered as black people. We were so broken down that we couldn't even see our own God-given beauty and dignity. We had to stand up in public and shout just to remember we were human.

But for so many of us, our identity got wrapped up in being black. The role of the black church was to speak out against oppression and get folks access to power. We didn't offer our children a new identity, so the ones who could leave the community did and those who couldn't leave got stuck in their anger and hopelessness.

The wound of the black church is an open wound, bleeding in public for everyone to see. Our communities are broken and the best thing we have to offer is a prosperity gospel that says, "Turn to your neighbor and tell them, 'I'm better than blessed.'" We've developed a church culture where we tell each other what we want to hear but don't take the time to listen to what God wants for our lives.

Everyone can see that our black families, communities and churches are broken. But as an evangelist to the white church, I've also learned to see the hidden wounds of white Christians. No one ever put a chain on another human being without tying the other end to themself. We know this. But it can be hard for white folks to see how race continues to hold them captive. This makes it hard for them to accept the freedom Jesus offers in God's kingdom.

Not long ago I was speaking to the students at Belhaven College, a wonderful Presbyterian school in Jackson, Mississippi. My son Spencer graduated from Belhaven, and I always love talking to the students there. On this particular day, after I preached about God's vision for reconciliation one of the professors walked me over to the dining hall for a talk-back session with the students. As we were walking, he celebrated how well the kids had received me and started talking about how far we've come with reconciliation. He told me how his church had just invited the first black man to preach in its pulpit. I could tell he was proud.

"You ought to be ashamed," I told him. "After more than a hundred years your church has finally found a black man you'll accept, and you want me to be happy about it?" I've been the first black man to preach in more churches than I can count. But I still can't believe how imperialistic white churches can be, celebrating "progress" when they finally get around to seeing that they might be able to learn something from a black person. I don't doubt the sincerity of that professor. But our conversation reminded me how race continues to hold white Christians captive.

One of the most lasting effects of racism on white churches is an intellectual wound that makes people think they'll do right if they believe right. So they put all of their emphasis on believing the right things. Preachers work so hard to get their doctrine right, and then they try to think of clever ways to get their congregations to sit and listen to their good theology. I ask them, "How are you helping your church learn to love?" And they tell me, "Well, if they're Christians they will love." But I've met a lot of Christians who don't know what love means. I talk to white Christians all the time who say, "I love black people. I had a black nanny growing up, and I really loved her." Love isn't just a good feeling. It's an action that requires conversion.

"Do not merely listen to the word, and so deceive yourselves," James says in his epistle. "Do what it says" (James 1:22). But so many white Christians today don't believe they can do anything—especially in the black community. They've caught on to the fact that white people have done wrong in the past, so they've decided not to do anything at all. They've bought into this idea that our cultures are so different we can't do anything together. I don't understand. General Motors doesn't believe in this radical cultural difference. They make the same commercials for us that they do for white people, and we buy more of their Cadillacs than anyone else. If ads can cross these racial walls, why can't the church?

Another thing I just don't understand is why the same white churches who think they are too culturally different to do anything in my black community send mission teams to Africa. Is the cultural barrier easier to cross in an airplane? We've let this world define us to the point that we don't trust God to transform us and make community possible across racial and economic lines. It's easy to give out of abundance and help the poor Africans "over there." But white Christians hesitate to cross the tracks in their own hometown and meet their brothers and sisters on the other side.

We have a seminary in Mississippi that was developed to provide pastors for rural churches when the denomination's seminary in Atlanta became too "liberal" for most of those churches. These country churches would send their children to the seminary in Atlanta, and the kids wouldn't come back. They would stay in Atlanta or go off to take a job in some other city. Their home churches thought it was because the students had become liberal. So the churches started a more conservative seminary right here in Mississippi. While the students are studying at the seminary, they serve these little country churches as student pastors.

I go over and talk to the student pastors at this conservative seminary every chance I get. But I don't talk to them so much about doctrine. I try to help them see that their education shouldn't make them condescending toward the poor people they're serving in these churches.

Poor white folks are in such a sad condition. No one likes them. Black folks don't like them because they're racist. Immigrants don't like them because they compete for jobs. White folks don't like them because they're failures. They don't have a Jesse Jackson or an Al Sharpton to fight for them. Poor white folks have been rejected by everyone; they're on their own.

If I have any regret about my own ministry, it's that I haven't done more with poor white people. Sometimes I go out into the country here in Mississippi on a food distribution day, which we usually have at a black church in the community. But I watch the poor white folks when they come. They're so ashamed. Their faces are turned down to the ground and they hardly say anything. No one likes them. Not even their pastors. I always ask the student pastors over at the seminary, "How can you win people you don't like?"

I think the Ku Klux Klan has been so powerful among poor whites because it offered them a community where they felt accepted when everyone else rejected them. Poor white people found some false sense of purpose and dignity in terrorizing us. I saw this in the officers who beat me in the Brandon County Jail. They didn't have much meaning in their lives, but they thought they were doing something important when they tortured me. Hurting me made them feel like somebody when everyone else said they were nobodies.

I really believe that the first truth God wants every one of us to know is that we are created in his image and therefore have inherent dignity. The Klan offered poor white people a sense of self-worth, but they still had to cover their faces with a hood when they paraded in public. Dignity that comes from terrorizing other people will never last. True dignity can't be about anything you do to prove yourself, even though we do have to stand up and affirm dignity when it is denied. In the end, dignity is a gift all of us receive from God.

Sin has messed us up so badly that we sometimes don't recognize that dignity in ourselves or in other people. This may be the deepest wound that any of us carries: our desperate need to know that we are loved for who we are. But Jesus came down from heaven and gave his life to show us how much God loves each one of us. Even while we were his enemies, Christ died for us. That's the greatest love you'll ever know, and it has the power to transform both our lives and our society.

DRIVING A WEDGE IN THE STATUS QUO

Jesus is the incarnation of God's love. "He himself is our peace," Ephesians 2:14 says. But Jesus also said he came into our world to disturb the peace—to drive a wedge into the divided society that holds us captive. "Do not suppose that I have come to bring peace to the earth," he says in Matthew's Gospel. "I did not come to bring peace, but a sword" (10:34). That sword is a wedge to interrupt the way things are, not a weapon to wield in defense of the status quo. Instead of continually seeking God's will for our lives and communities, we hold the Holy Spirit captive to our own desires—our selfish materialistic desires. We see this in the prosperity gospel running rampant through the church today. The church is called to be the prophetic voice in response to society; that's what we see in the model Jesus provided.

I love the sermons in the book of Acts. The apostles quoted the Scriptures as the Holy Spirit helped them remember and they applied the words they had heard from Jesus to their lives. Stephen's sermon before the Sanhedrin is one of my favorites. He retells the whole story of Israel, starting all the way back at Abraham. As he tells the story, he points out to the Sanhedrin how God's people have been slow to believe all along. The Jewish leaders at that time wanted to blame their problems on outside influences. They said that everything would be all right if Jews could just purge their tradition of the Gentile influence that was corrupting it.

But Stephen reminded those Bible scholars how God's people had refused to obey him in the wilderness. He told them Israel hadn't listened to the prophets of old. He pointed out that they invested all their money and energy in keeping up the temple, but "the Most High does not live in houses made by human hands" (Acts 7:48). Stephen knew that God had called Abraham from the very beginning to be a blessing to all the nations. Israel needed those outsiders, and Jesus had thrown open the doors to everyone. But the Sanhedrin wouldn't hear it. They'd killed Jesus, and when Stephen told them the truth, they killed him too.

Acts says that the people who witnessed the stoning of Stephen "laid their coats at the feet of a young man named Saul" (7:58). Saul inherited this religion that feared the outsider and used violence to guard the status quo. He became a persecutor of the early church because he believed that God needed him to root out this new movement and purge Judaism of outside influences. But on the road to Damascus, God confronted Saul's madness with his love and asked him, "Why do you persecute me?" God interrupted Saul and made him into a troublemaker for the kingdom.

I believe God interrupts us with his love. So often when we're interrupted, we get mad. I know what it feels like to be mad at God. When my son Spencer died, I was mad at God. Spencer had given his whole life to reconciliation, and I was so proud of him. He married Nancy, a white woman, and they shared their lives with an integrated community of Christians at Antioch House. With his friend Chris Rice, Spencer had led a national reconciliation ministry. I remember standing there at his funeral, praying and telling God I was mad. A verse of Scripture came into my mind: "unless a kernel of wheat falls to the ground and dies, it remains only a single seed." I thought about that verse, and I remembered the little poem by Jim Elliot: "He is no fool who gives what he cannot keep to gain what he cannot lose." God was speaking to me, and the scales fell off my eyes.

I prayed and said, "God, Spencer was a reconciler. He gave his life trying to bridge the racial divide in this country. I've been saying you took him, Lord, but he laid down his life willingly for you. And I want to release him. I want to give him back to you, God." I said that prayer and knew that God had interrupted me with his love. God showed me through Spencer's death that

I needed to give the rest of my life to reconciliation right here in West Jackson where Spencer was trying to do it. Whatever the cost, I needed to carry on the work that he'd been called to do.

His work was the same work Paul had been called to on the Damascus Road—the work of proclaiming reconciliation for all people in Jesus Christ. From the very beginning of God's movement in the world, God has been interrupting people with his love—disturbing our false peace in order to make real peace possible. Jesus drives a wedge in the status quo to create space for something new. If we have ears to hear, the invitation is open for each of us: come and be part of the beloved community that God makes possible in Jesus Christ.

CALL TO COMMITMENT

I believe the work of my latter years is to make reconciliation a discipleship issue for the church. When I was first called into the ministry, God gave me a ministry of communicating his love to men in prison and poor children in Mississippi, and I still love that work. I love to stand out at the bus stop when the kids are getting off for our after-school program and hear them shout, "Hey, Grandpa Perkins!" Through our work in Mendenhall in the sixties and seventies, God gave me a vision for Christian community development, and it has been one of the greatest joys of my life to see the "three Rs" method spread through the more than six hundred member organizations of the Christian Community Development Organization.[1] Since I published *Let Justice Roll Down* and *With Justice for All*, we've seen a huge shift in evangelical churches; the division between personal faith and social action has been bridged by a new generation. It's so wonderful to see justice becoming a discipleship issue for evangelicals.

But in these latter days of my ministry, God is calling me to help churches see and incorporate reconciliation as an essential part of discipleship. The captivity of the church to our culture has left us so divided. And we think division is natural. We think the traditions we've inherited from our forebears are the way things have to be. But Jesus came to drive a wedge in the status quo and create spaces where new life can happen. "Anyone who loves their father or mother more than me is not worthy of me," Jesus said; "anyone who loves a son or daughter more than me is not worthy of me. Whoever does not take up their cross and follow me is not worthy of me" (Matthew 10:37-38). The call to reconciliation is a call to commitment—to take up the cross and give ourselves to *this* community in *this* place. The world needs a church that does something to interrupt business as usual where we are.

The cultural captivity of the church means we aren't calling people to much of anything. Sure, we have meetings where people can hear a sermon that makes them feel better or come and get their praise on. We have programs that advocate for homeless people or raise money to feed the hungry. We even have prophets and radical witnesses whom we praise for living among the poor or risking their lives to make peace in conflictive situations. But what does the church really ask of most of us? What kind of commitment is required for you to join the congregation you're part of?

I'm just an amateur historian, but one thing I've learned from my own experience and from my study of history is that every good movement calls people to commitment. Every good movement inspires each individual to make sacrifices for the greater good. Every good movement invites people into something greater than themselves—something they would not be foolish to sacrifice everything for. Jesus said, "Again, the kingdom of heaven is like a merchant looking for fine pearls. When he found one of great value, he went away and sold everything he had and bought it" (Matthew 13:45-46). I believe the ministry of reconciliation is about calling people to give everything for God's vision of a church where we love one another across society's dividing lines. My son showed me that this ministry can cost you your life. But from the seed that he sowed, I have seen the Spencer Perkins Center spring up. I believe its fruit will be thousands of Christians who give themselves and their resources to true reconciliation in a new era.

It's been more than forty years since Martin Luther King Jr. was killed and the Civil Rights movement faded away. In those days, we worked hard for integration, the right to vote, access to education and basic dignity. It was such an important time in my life—an important time for everyone in this country. But more than forty years later, we see that the work we're called to has changed. So many of the responses to the Civil Rights struggle made by the government did not affirm the dignity of black men. The black man is being defined by our society as a "baby's daddy" instead of a father. We see the effects in the black population—

family and children, men and women. Our work, forty years later, is to build up the black man.

In the Bible, forty is an important number. Israel wandered in the wilderness for forty years. Jesus was in the desert for forty days. God used these measures of forty to prepare his people and his Son for something new. I believe that's what God has been doing for these past forty years. He has been tilling the soil, scattering the seed and preparing the church for a new thing. We're on the verge of a new Christianity, and it so excites me to see it.

Dietrich Bonhoeffer's *The Cost of Discipleship* has always been such an important book to me. It challenged us to go beyond "cheap grace" and take seriously Jesus' call to take up our cross and follow him in the way of the kingdom. Of course, Bonhoeffer wrote his book in Nazi Germany, where he could see how the church he knew was held captive by the culture of his day. Bonhoeffer tried to resist Hitler as part of the Confessing Church and ultimately gave his life in an attempt to stop Hitler.

I love Bonhoeffer's book and I so respect him as a witness, but when I think about his situation and ours, I feel sad for Bonhoeffer. He was so alone. He heard the call to commitment, but in the end it was too little, too late. Bonhoeffer died as a lonely witness, frustrated by a church that had largely abandoned him.

Around the same time Bonhoeffer was writing *The Cost of Discipleship,* a little group of people who would later call themselves the Bruderhof started meeting to talk about what it might mean to live the Sermon on the Mount together as God's people. In the little village of Sannerz, they declared that they wanted to be "part of the stream of the Spirit that began at Pentecost" and live together in a "genuine school of life" to demonstrate "that a life of justice and forgiveness and unity is possible today."[2] When I look back on the church in Nazi Germany, it seems to me that the Bruderhof did as much as Bonhoeffer to interrupt the madness and show another way.

When the Nazis realized what these Christians were up to, they ran them out of Germany. The Bruderhof became a people without a home, and eventually found their way to the United States in the 1950s. When the Civil Rights movement came to Mississippi, a number of Bruderhof people came down to help us. And after the movement moved on, they kept coming. I've always been impressed by their commitment to follow Jesus and live the kingdom out here on earth as it is in heaven.

That's the commitment we're going to need if we're going to make reconciliation a discipleship issue for the church today. And I'm so excited to see that commitment now among the young people I meet all around the country. They want more from the church, and they're willing to give themselves to the hard work of community in places like West Jackson. They are becoming the church we've prayed for, and it's such a joy to see it.

Interrupting the status quo can't just be the work of super-Christians or the calling of a few. Jesus wants us to become communities of believers who give ourselves in service to one another as a new family in the world. We can't be held captive by the traditions of our parents or by fear and concern for our children. Each of us has to be willing to take up our cross and follow Jesus across the dividing lines of our world. We're not called to be heroes. We're called to commitment where we are. We're called to join God's movement and enjoy the life we were made for together with all of God's children.

3

The Power of True Conversion

CHARLES MARSH

*I*n 1980 I finished college in Massachusetts, and through a series of circumstances having little to do with interest in racial justice, I accepted a job for the summer in the inner city of Atlanta. In preparation for the work, I was asked to read John Perkins's memoir, *Let Justice Roll Down*. While vacationing after graduation, I picked up the book. Page one, opening paragraphs:

> I remember when it happened like it was yesterday. Only it wasn't yesterday. It was summer 1946. The war was over, and it was cotton-picking time in New Hebron.
>
> That summer of 1946 was a hot one. Real hot—with a limp kind of heat that lay over the land like a blanket.
>
> And that was when it happened.

That was the summer Perkins's brother Clyde returned from

the war as a military hero with a Purple Heart. And that was the summer Perkins watched Clyde bleed to death after being shot twice in the chest at point-blank range by the town's white deputy. I was deeply moved and saddened by the story.

I called Perkins from the cottage in North Carolina where I was staying and told him I was coming to Jackson the next weekend. I hoped we could get together for a visit. I also told him I was enjoying his book and that I was sure it would prepare me well for my summer in the inner city.

Perkins, in his friendly manner, said that he would be happy to meet with me and that I should just call him when I got to town. He asked me what the weather was like in North Carolina. A cool breeze was blowing down the mountainside, and I was sitting in a rocking chair on the screen porch wearing a sweatshirt. He sighed and said I'd better enjoy it while I could, because in Mississippi the heat was already sticking in the air. Ninety degrees, and not even June.

"You have family in Mississippi?" he asked.

"Yes sir. My grandmother lives over by Belhaven College." I didn't tell him about the other grandparents, the ones who had fled to the all-white trailer park in the new subdivision south of town called Plantation Shores—the ones who had lived on Buena Vista Boulevard, a block away from the Perkins's home in West Jackson, but who had left his neighborhood the same summer he moved in.

"My mom and dad are from Jackson," I added. "So it kind of feels like home to me."

"Well, I'm sure we'll have a lot to talk about."

When I got to town I called Perkins from a pay phone at a convenience store. My grandmother in Jackson had not moved to the suburbs, but that was not because she held more progressive views on race. Though Nana was a remarkable woman, she would have thrown a fit—and possibly a kitchen utensil—had she known that I was arranging a visit with a black pastor and activist. She still could not come to terms with the scandalous fact that her deceased husband had oftentimes greeted a Negro with a handshake. Some of her more mischievous grandchildren, just for the fun of watching her explode, would espouse the virtues of affirmative action and school desegregation. When my oldest cousin from Newellton, Louisiana, told her I was dating a black girl in Massachusetts, she called me in my dorm to get an explanation. (I did not tell her that the rumor was untrue.)

Contrary to what my New England classmates may have thought about my southern romanticism, in Mississippi in 1980 you could still be considered a liberal for liking *Sanford and Son.* In fact, Mississippi in 1980 was not too different from Mississippi in 1970 as far as I could tell. On one of my first mornings in Jackson, I was lying on the coach in my grandmother's house watching *The Phil Donahue Show* when the program suddenly went blank. A flashing message appeared, indicating to viewers that the station was experiencing technical difficulties. The moment the broadcasting of the show stopped, a black sociology professor from Atlanta was giving a lecture on white racism in America on the TV screen. His name was Charles King, and he stood in front of a chalkboard furiously drawing flow charts and graphs and writing down terms to make his case: "WHITE SUPREMACY." "SOCIAL SEGREGATION." Here was the way racism traversed the cruel centuries on its way toward oppression, slavery and genocide, his markings on the board said.

King was a tall, imposing figure. He quoted Marx. He quoted Elijah Muhammad. He quoted Martin Luther King Jr. and the prophet Amos. He said he was speaking to all white Americans—southerners and northerners, Christians and Jews, Democrats and Republicans. He told us we lived in a land that despised its poor and its minorities. He told us that America was born and bred on white supremacy and that nothing short of a scorched-earth revolution would change it. But after a few minutes along these lines, Charles King was not talking to anybody in Mississippi.

Throughout the long sorry years of massive white resistance to civil rights for blacks, the message "Sorry, Cable Trouble," was a familiar sight on Jackson television screens. The strange ritual began on September 12, 1955, when the civil rights attorney Thurgood Marshall appeared on the *Today* show to discuss school desegregation. In the middle of the interview, Jackson's NBC affiliate, WLBT, interrupted the broadcast with a "Cable Difficulty" message. The station manager later acknowledged at a Citizens' Council meeting that he had "pulled the plug" on Thurgood Marshall—and he received a hearty round of applause for his efforts in protecting the Magnolia State against "Negro propaganda."

Over the next decade, Jackson's two network affiliates made

it a matter of policy to preempt any program that mentioned the topic of race. As a result, most Mississippians were unable to see television shows that discussed the changing times in Dixie. Even the presence of a black contestant in the Miss America pageant, or a black fullback running the option for USC, seemed provocative and unsettling.

In my grandmother's English Tudor cottage on Fairview Street near Belhaven College, Eudora Welty's *One Writer's Beginnings* and *Foxe's Book of Martyrs* by John Foxe rested on a bookshelf in the front hallway. There were tattered volumes of John Calvin, F. B. Meyer and C. S. Lewis—good evangelical fare. And there among them, Claude Bowers's *The Tragic Era* as well as *Black Monday* by Tom Brady, the Princeton-educated judge who wrote, "The Northern negroes are determined to mongrelize America!" From this "fallen paradise," as Walker Percy once described his adopted state, I found myself sneaking away to a convenience store to call John Perkins.

WAKING UP ON THE WAY

Perkins asked me to pick him up around five o'clock in the afternoon. He wanted me to drive him to Yazoo City where he was scheduled to speak at a youth rally. I was a little uneasy about the assignment. Mickey Schwerner's burned-out station wagon was the only image in my head of blacks and whites driving together along country roads in Mississippi. In fact, aside from a few times in high school when I drove a black teammate home after bas- ketball practice, I had never been in the same car with a black

ℓ– wow

57

person. Perkins's idea was that we would talk on the way up—which was about an hour's drive—and then stop at Shoney's on the ride home for a piece of their famous hot fudge cake.

Five minutes north of the county line, Perkins fell into a deep sleep, his body folding into the space between the seat and the door of the rental car. He was exhausted. And I drove northeast with no map and no conception of where Yazoo City lay in the geography of the Mississippi Delta. I had been there once, I think, to play in a junior high basketball tournament, but that didn't help me now, of course. I was completely lost. But I couldn't bring myself to wake Perkins up. Think about it (and I sure did): here next to me slept—and snored—a black man who, except for the grace of God, had every reason to choke the life out of me. Here was a "modern saint," as the evangelical U.S. senator Mark Hatfield had called him. I knew that just days earlier he had returned from a grueling trip to Haiti, where he had visited slum areas throughout the country, sharing his Christian community development vision with religious leaders and community organizers.

Besides that, I knew from his memoir that Perkins had the reputation of a tireless worker. And here I was, a white, fifth-generation Mississippian whose great-great-grandfather had been a founding member of the Ku Klux Klan. I had no intention of interrupting Perkins's much-needed rest. So on I drove, as the late afternoon light faded. And still no sign of Yazoo City. I don't know how far I would have gone had I not needed to stop for gas. In a town called Belzoni, under the bright lights of a Shell station, Perkins woke up.

"I guess I fell asleep, didn't I?" He seemed confused by my presence at the wheel of the car. "Where are we?" he yawned.

"Belzoni. I must have missed Yazoo City."

He looked at his watch. "We won't make it to the youth rally."

"I'm so sorry," I said. "I didn't want to wake you up. I didn't know what to do."

"That's okay." He shrugged. "I didn't really want to talk to those kids anyway." Then Perkins smiled and said, "Let's drive back to Jackson get some hot fudge cake at Shoney's."

On the ride back, Perkins talked about his favorite writers. He liked Margaret Walker above all others, the Jackson State professor whose Civil War novel, *Jubilee*, had reached the *New York Times* bestseller list. Richard Wright was also a favorite, but he confessed that Wright's recollections of his childhood in Mississippi sometimes proved difficult to read, given the brutal similarities of their stories. I told Perkins I had read Alice Walker's *The Third Life of Grange Copeland* just the week before, and he seemed excited. He too liked Alice Walker; he'd read *Meridian* as well as her poetry, and liked her writings a lot, though he was saddened to hear somewhere that she had given up Christianity.

Perkins also talked about his children. His son Spencer had graduated the previous year from Belhaven College and was now working in California.

By the time we got to the restaurant, I was not only feeling comfortable in his presence but also empowered by it. As the hostess led us to our seats, between rows of red patent-leather booths filled with white folks out for the evening, I felt eyes turning toward us—and it felt great. I had never been in this situation before, flaunting conventional racial customs in a public place with one of the state's best-known inside agitators—and a Bible-believing Christian to boot. We sat at our booth and drank coffee until after midnight, eating the hot fudge cake and, later, a plate of pancakes and fried eggs, if I'm not mistaken.

I wanted to know how the white churches in Jackson had responded to Perkins's work at Voice of Calvary. His simple answer—they hadn't responded at all—surprised me. He seemed puzzled when I asked why this was so.

"You tell me," he said.

"I really don't know," I replied.

"Well, why are you working in the inner city this summer?"

"I believe God wants me there," was all I could say, and I wasn't even sure what that meant. (I didn't tell him that a beautiful, young, Presbyterian minister's daughter was also working there, and that my real motivation was to get to know Karen Wright a whole lot better. As it turns out, I did get to know her a lot better. We've been married since 1982.)

"Then I guess that's why the white churches don't care about poor black neighborhoods. They don't think God wants them there. Most of the preachers know better, but they're scared to tell the truth. So nothing really changes in the way white people think about blacks."

As I drove Perkins home, I told him about my grandmother in

Belhaven. "You know, Dr. Perkins, the first thing she does every morning is open up her Bible and read her devotions. There's a worn-out chair in her bedroom she likes to sit in. She'll turn the chair toward the window so she can look out at the garden. Nana will study that Bible for hours—an old red Scofield edition. She'll gaze down through her magnifying glass at the pages, underlining sentences and words in red pencils, green pencils, blue pencils. She'll pray a while. She'll listen to a sermon on tape—maybe one of my father's, or David Dehann, or some Reformed Bible teacher. But she won't give an inch on her racial views. She thinks Martin Luther King Jr. was nothing but a troublemaker."

"He was a troublemaker, wasn't he?" Perkins said.

"I've heard her say that slavery wasn't a bad thing. Lots of blacks had it good then, better than they do now."

I had never told anyone—certainly not a black man—about my grandmother's racial views. I felt like I had come clean with a dirty secret, and Perkins was my confessor. But his response was bewildering. Or perhaps it was just the kind of response a confessor should make.

"What does she grow in her garden?" he asked.

"What do you mean?"

"What does she grow? Cucumbers, squash, mint, tomatoes? I have the sweetest tomatoes in my garden this summer. You can eat them like apples. Your grandmother like tomato sandwiches? I bet she does. Let me ask you another question: does she like blueberries? I love blueberries," the then fifty-year-old

Perkins said, and in great detail he described all the ways he loved to eat blueberries: freshly picked, over ice cream, in blueberry pie. "I always keep blueberries in my refrigerator. When we get to the house, I'm gonna give you a bag of blueberries, and I want you to take them to your grandmother and tell her they're a gift from me."

I didn't realize then what Perkins was showing me, but I see now that those blueberries were something like an altar call—the kind of gift that makes you a giver and marks you as a new kind of person. I haven't been quite the same since I accepted those blueberries.

Conversions We Forget

More than a decade later, while I was doing field research for my book *God's Long Summer,* Karen and I visited the small town of Ruleville, Mississippi. On a sweltering July morning we drove northwest from Jackson, up the old State Highway 49 to Yazoo City that I had traveled years earlier with Dr. Perkins. We drove through the dense alluvial textures of the southern summer in search of the grave of Mrs. Fannie Lou Hamer, the lady in a homespun dress who became the prophetic voice of poor African Americans in the rural South.

In time the hilly terrain gave way to the flat, rich fields of the Delta, and we entered the town of Belzoni. Rather than turn around at the Shell station this time, we stopped for a while at the International Catfish Museum, claiming our souvenir baseball caps and coffee cups and having our photo taken in front of the forty-foot catfish sculpture erected outside in the garden. As we drove on toward Ruleville, we passed billboards honoring many famous locals—Jim Henson, the creator of the Muppets; Mary Lou somebody, once a Miss America; and Lamar Fontaine, a Confederate poet enshrined in downtown Clarksdale. But the faded sign at the city limits of Ruleville greeted us only with the news that the Fighting Tigers had won the 2-A football title some years back—and that's nothing to laugh about. Still, you had to know in advance that one of the great prophetic voices of the rural South had lived her life and died here.

In 1962 at the age of forty-four, Fannie Lou Hamer left the cotton fields "to work for Jesus" (as he put it) in civil rights activism. At a worship service one night in her little Baptist church in Sunflower County she heard a sermon by James Bevel, one of Martin Luther King Jr.'s young foot soldiers in the Southern Christian Leadership Conference, who had preached on discerning the signs of the times. In a moment of clarity and conviction, Hamer's eyes were opened to see in the burgeoning struggle for black equality under the law nothing less than the moving of the Spirit toward freedom.

It was a remarkable moment for a woman who'd worked her entire life as a sharecropper on a Marlowe plantation. Since the age of seven, she had been out in the fields picking cotton with her fourteen brothers and five sisters, the family working hard days and still not making enough money to live on. (Plantation owners, always in need of cheap labor, encouraged poor mothers to have lots of children.) From the first days of planting in early April to the chopping of weeds under the hot sun of June and

July to the picking of the completed harvest in the frosty mornings of October and November, Mrs. Hamer and the other field hands worked long hard days. They worked from the gray hour before sunrise until long after darkness had descended—from "cain't to cain't" as one local person described it: "cain't see in the mornin' 'cause it's too *early* 'til cain't see at night 'cause it's too *late*." The work was monotonous and humiliating. "Oh Lord, you know just how I feel," Mrs. Hamer might drag out as she slowly walked a long row of cotton, filling her sack for what must have seemed the thousandth time.

Like her mother and father before her, and her slave ancestors before them, Mrs. Hamer had looked on the long rows of cotton as the only future white Mississippi would afford black folks in the Delta. But James Bevel's sermon, followed by a talk on the constitutional right to vote, spoke directly to her deepest longings for dignity and justice.

During the electrifying rally that went late into the evening, Hamer's imagination was awakened by new spiritual and moral energies. By the end of the night, she felt called to change her life, and *readied* to step out on God's promise to bless. "When they asked for those to raise their hands who'd go down to the courthouse the next day, I raised mine. Had it up as high as I could get it. I guess if I'd had any sense I'd a-been a little scared, but what was the point of being scared. The only thing [the whites] could do was kill me and it seemed like they'd been trying to do that a little bit at a time for as long as I could remember."[1]

Mrs. Hamer's life from that moment until she died in poverty in 1977 mirrored her conviction that God takes worldly form in human lives empowered by love. She gave voice to an exuberant Christian spirituality, evangelical in the best sense of the word, and embodied a robust and disciplined love of Jesus of Nazareth—indeed, of the whole miraculous story of his life, death and resurrection. At the same time, her love was a great big love, open to anyone who cared for the weak and the poor. She emerged as the prophetic voice of poor black Mississippians and a true ambassador of reconciliation.

Mrs. Hamer sometimes spoke of the Civil Rights movement as a welcoming table, the kind that might be found beside a rural Baptist church, where on special Sundays and dinners-on-the-ground, the abundant riches of southern cooking would be spread out for everyone to enjoy—even Governor Ross Barnett and Senator James O. Eastland, though they would need to learn some manners.[2] "Christ was a revolutionary person, out there where it's happening," she said. "That's what God is all about, and that's where I get my strength."[3] Mrs. Hamer's Christianity, like the faith of the other movement mothers and fathers, was exuberantly Christian in its singing and testifying, and yet equally generous to non-Christian fellow travelers.

If you go in search of her grave, as my wife and I did that hot summer day years ago, you will find it in a large field behind an elementary school. Although there is now a historical marker and some commemoration of her life and witness, she died in poverty on March 14, 1977, suffering in the last years of her life; she battled a devastating assault of cancer, heart disease and diabetes, along with severe mental strain and depression. Her lack of disability income intensified the stress, along with inconsistent health care. Similar to so many of the church's prophets, she died without honor in her hometown.

Like her friend John Perkins, Mrs. Hamer has helped me see what true conversion looks like.

"When we meet a saint we are not discovering . . . an ideal, lived and realized, which had already been formed within us," wrote the twentieth-century theologian Henri de Lubac. "A saint is not the perfection of humanity—or the superman—incarnate in a particular man. The marvel is of a different order. What we find is a new life, a new sphere of existence, with unsuspected depths—but also with a resonance hitherto unknown to us and now at last revealed."[4] John Perkins and Mrs. Hamer offer us that kind of witness. A quarter-century after meeting Perkins, I keep thinking about those blueberries—the grace to offer a gift, the invitation to taste the sweetness of blueberries, even, or especially, in the face of those who have been agents of exclusion. The astonishing life and legacy of John Perkins is the story of a Christian who finds the strength to keep the arms of mercy and reconciliation open.[5]

I have spent much of the past ten years researching and writing and thinking theologically about the Civil Rights movement in the South. And I have come to see that so many of the best stories of that remarkable Pentecostal event that changed our nation and made us a better people are the smaller stories—the stories of everyday bravery and long-forgotten failures, stories of quiet compassion and unreflective acts of kindness. So many of the best ones are about people like Fannie Lou Hamer and John Perkins. These stories about blueberries and welcoming tables are important because they, like the lives of all saints, help each of us hear the invitation to join God's movement where we are. Henri de Lubac might have been describing Perkins's gift of blueberries for my Nana when he wrote of the effect saints have on us: "All of a sudden the universe seems different; it is the stage of a vast drama, and we, at its heart, are compelled to play our part."[6]

A More Compelling Church

Occasionally in one of my courses on modern religious thought I assign late writings by the philosopher Friedrich Nietzsche, sections from *Thus Spake Zarathustra* or the short book called *The Antichrist*. Nietzsche was the nineteenth-century sage whose books make today's New Atheists look like complete wimps. He waged dramatic war against Christianity and its tendency to suffocate life and inhibit passion. Christianity, he said, is a religion of "everything low and botched."

"Whoever had the blood of theologians in his veins," Nietzsche wrote in *The Antichrist*, "stands from the start in a false and dishonest position to all things."[7] He claimed that the Christian religion promotes a "deadly hostility to reality" and turns the spirit of life into fear and suspicion, joy into self-loathing, passion into paranoia. Much of Nietzsche's criticism of the church he knew is striking in its condemnation of Christianity in our own day. But one particular sentence from his discourse "On Priests" in *Thus Spake Zarathustra* continues to challenge me, even after I have come to terms with its more complex meanings: "They will have to sing better songs before I shall believe in their redeemer."[8] His criticism of Christianity is a complex one, and I don't want to simplify it for my own purposes here. But in a profound sense, his hope has become the credo of my writing life: to make a space in language for Christian honesty and for singing beautiful songs. There is no song more beautiful than that of the love of God poured out for humanity in the redeeming and reconciling gift of Jesus Christ.

Most of my students who have left the faith have left not because they read Kant's critique of the ontological and cosmological arguments for the existence of God, but because they have listened to Christians in hope of hearing beautiful songs and have instead heard something thin and shrill. But the church has beautiful songs to sing. Fannie Lou Hamer and John Perkins know our best songs and have sung them with their lives. And when we listen closely, we can hear the songs of other men and women who work day in and day out in inauspicious places to bring healing to the broken and blistered world. They are carried and strengthened and nourished by deep spiritual waters. That is certainly what I have heard in my listening to the history of the Civil Rights movement.

Mrs. Victoria Gray Adams, a field director for SNCC and later a campus minister at Virginia State University, and a dear friend of mine, called the Civil Rights movement an "enfleshened church."[9] Growing out of a rich theological tradition, this church pursued a form of Christian discipleship that was life-affirming, socially transformative and existentially demanding. For SNCC, organizing meant listening with humility to the concerns of local people, but not in order to make poverty normative. Organizing for power meant protecting and advancing the interests of poor people by creating networks to focus on urgent social needs. It meant transforming the material conditions of impoverished communities. It meant going into a distressed community in the spirit of servanthood, seeking to discern the needs of the people. The Christian vision of beloved community sustained these disciplines of listening, discernment, and action.

With a wonderfully eclectic and generous spirit, SNCC embodied a theology for radicals. Its Christian commitments were often subtle and unstated in the day-to-day work of organizing, yet its theology for radicals allowed itself to be invigorated with the rough-hewn wisdom and unguarded testimonials of the trained and the untrained. John Lewis, a freedom rider and chairman of SNCC, described the movement's moral shape as "nothing less than the Christian concept of the Kingdom of God on earth," as a "redemptive society" that heals social wounds and divisions.[10] Beloved community gave expression to all that Lewis was longing for as a young seminarian devoted to the venture of making the teachings of Jesus come alive in the towns and hamlets of the segregated South.

SNCC's founding mothers and fathers were almost all radical Christians, exuberantly faithful people motivated by diverse theological sources combined in unusual—sometimes even exotic—ways according to the demands of the situation. Theological existentialism, holiness fervor, contemplative asceticism, social gospel idealism, Protestant liberal hope and even some good old-fashioned otherworldliness were all part of the mix. But without a doubt, faith was the driving force behind the most compelling social movement in this nation's history. True conversion didn't only change lives. It transformed society.

The existence of a compelling Christian witness in our time does not depend on our access to the White House, the size of our churches or the cultural relevance of our pastors. It depends, instead, on our ability to sing better songs with our lives. True conversion is always personal, but it is never solely about the individual who experiences God's love and knows the good news of salvation. True conversion is about learning to sing songs in which our life harmonizes with others'—even the lives of those least like us—and swells into a joyful and irresistible chorus.

Trinitarian theology teaches us that our God, who is One, exists eternally as three Persons united in a never-ending dance of self-giving love. To be baptized into the body of Christ is to get swept up in this dance right here on earth—to be part of "the world of God breaking through from its self-contained holiness and appearing in secular life," as Karl Barth once wrote.[11] We pay attention to the lived theology of people like John Perkins because it helps us see what beloved community can look like in the broken places of our world. Like all saints, Perkins points beyond himself to a community and beyond that community to God's great movement, of which Perkins's witness is a part. Like any beautiful song, his voice blends with that of Fannie Lou Hamer and countless others in a way that makes each of us say, "Because of God's amazing grace I can sing this song too."

4

The Next Great Awakening

JOHN M. PERKINS

The job of an evangelist is to connect God's good news with people's deep yearnings. Revival movements are always about connecting the gospel to a cause. Frederick Douglass had been a slave, so he preached against human bondage and turned abolition into a cause for people. William Wilberforce was likewise a champion for the abolition of slavery. Revivalist Charles Finney saw the class system developing during industrialization and connected Jesus' good news for the poor with a movement for social change. In fact, the altar call was invented by him. He asked people to come forward and give their lives to Jesus, but he also invited them to give themselves to a cause. That's what the altar call was about. There was work to be done in the movement, and those people who responded were saying, "You can call on me." They were enlisting as foot soldiers in a campaign for the kingdom of God.

As I travel around the country and talk to young people, I hear a new yearning coming out of this generation. People say it in different ways, but it seems to me that they're all looking for authentic relationship. Our society is broken and our culture has been stretched so thin by consumerism and exploitation that people don't feel like anyone knows who they are. They're busy and they're always around people, but it's almost like everyone is in their own little bubble, floating through the world on a sea they can't control. Maybe the little bubbles bump into each other every now and then, but it feels like everything depends on the wind and the waves. People feel alone in a world of chance, and they're desperate for relationships that they know are real.

To preach the gospel of Jesus Christ today, we've got to invite people into authentic relationships where they can be restored to a beloved community and work for the common good. The economists say that self-preservation is the first law of human nature, but I don't believe it. It's just not true. The most basic human instinct is to protect your children—to give yourself to something greater than yourself. We've been so dehumanized by this world's system that we think it's natural to live for ourselves alone. But it's not. God wants to restore us to the authentic relationships we were made for. That's what reconciliation is all about.

We are made in the image of God. We've got a Father who loves us and who created us for real relationship. But sin has separated us from authentic relationships. It has put up these walls around us; it keeps us from knowing God and from being known by other people. The good news, though, is that Jesus has broken down the walls. "For he himself is our peace," Ephesians says, "who has . . . destroyed the barrier, the dividing wall of hostility" (2:14). The Bible says that God's whole purpose in Jesus was to create a new community "and in one body to reconcile . . . [us] to God through the cross" (2:16). God reconciles us to himself as he restores us to authentic relationship with our neighbors and enemies through the cross. That is the good news of Jesus Christ.

Evangelism for the next great awakening is going to have to be more about discipling people into a new kind of relationship than about creating a "born again" experience or building institutions. I'm not against experiences or institutions. We need those things too. But if the gospel is going to connect with the deep yearning of this generation, we're going to have to learn how to invite people into authentic relationships. Thankfully, that's what a lot of the Bible is about.

LEARNING TO LOVE LIKE JESUS

Christians have spent a lot of time talking about who Jesus is without paying attention to how he lived. I believe in Jesus' virgin birth. I believe that he is fully God and fully human. I know that Jesus died to pay the debt for my sin and that his resurrection is the ultimate victory over the power of death.

Jesus is my Savior, but he is also my Lord and Teacher. I hear him say "Follow me" to the disciples, and I know he's talking to me. It's important to know who Jesus is. But it's just as important to know how he lived and what kind of life he calls us into. When Jesus says "Follow me," he's inviting us to learn God's way of working in the world. He's also modeling for us the best way to invite others into the kingdom.

I don't think we've paid enough attention to Jesus' model of leadership development. His public ministry wasn't that long— just three-and-a-half years—and he spent most of that time discipling twelve men who weren't important in that society. The disciples weren't young scholars preparing for positions in synagogues. They weren't children of the political elite preparing to lead. They were fishermen and tax collectors and failed revolutionaries. They were like so many of the young people in my neighborhood—tossed aside as rejects by society. But Jesus invested his whole ministry in them. He didn't do anything else with his time here on earth. He didn't start an organization or build up an institution. Jesus invested God's love in authentic relationship with broken people who were created in God's image.

We're so impressed by programs and big events that we miss the genius of Jesus' model. But over the years I've noticed that anywhere there's a little sign of the supernatural, people will find it. You don't have to advertise it. People are so hungry for deeper connection that they'll go down to Mexico or over to Europe to see a smudge on a window that looks like Jesus' face.

That's how it was with Jesus and people when he was on earth. He didn't set out to draw big crowds. He wanted to love a handful of people well and trust God to use that. He evangelized by loving broken people like they had never been loved before. That's all Jesus was about—and the word about him got out pretty fast. When he saw people who were crushed by sickness and exploitation, Jesus healed them. He healed the woman with the issue of blood because he loved her. He healed the man who'd been lying beside a pool most of his life because he loved him. Jesus healed people because he loved them, not because he wanted to draw a crowd.

One of our biggest problems as Christians is that we want the miracle without the love. We want to see the kind of healing Jesus brought, but we don't want to learn Jesus' way of loving broken people. Jesus performed signs and wonders here on earth, but he was also clear that the sign of the church ought to be love: "By this everyone will know that you are my disciples, if you love one another" (John 13:35). Love is supposed to be the abiding sign of the church. I don't think we can have beloved communities until we learn to love like Jesus loves and make that our main plan for sharing the gospel.

I didn't set out to start a national association of Christian community development organizations. We've been gathering annually now for twenty years as the Christian Community Development Association (CCDA), and I'm so proud of the work all our member organizations are doing. But it amazes me every year to look out there and see thousands of people who are coming to hear me talk about community development. I didn't set out to start a movement. I wanted to love people. I wanted to love the young people of Mendenhall because Jesus had transformed me with his love. Somehow, the word got out. And people came. God's love is powerful. We can't underestimate the importance of learning to love like Jesus loves.

INDIGENOUS LEADERSHIP DEVELOPMENT

Paul picked up on Jesus' method of indigenous leadership development. He understood what Jesus had really been about. Authentic relationship became the basis for his church-planting strategy. You can see it in his letters to Timothy: "You then, my son," Paul wrote, "be strong in the grace that is in Christ Jesus" (2 Timothy 2:1). Timothy probably grew up without a father. He may have even been born out of wedlock. His mother, Eunice, and his grandmother Lois taught him the story of God's people, but Paul was a father figure to Timothy. Paul connected the faith of Timothy's mother with his felt need for authentic relationship. And Timothy became a leader in God's movement to heal the world through the church.

Paul's words to Timothy are such embracing words. "My son," he calls him. Paul has shared the good news of Jesus with Timothy by discipling him into a family where he knows he is loved. This is what I do with our kids in my neighborhood. I tell them, "I love you." One of our little girls always says, "I know, Grandpa Perkins, but you can say it again." I don't want anyone to doubt that they are loved for who they are. That's the most basic thing they need to get inside of themselves. They need to know they're loved so they can go on and do something else.

Paul calls Timothy "my son," and then he tells him to "be strong in the grace that is in Christ Jesus." I think Paul used that word *grace* as the all-encompassing word to describe the new kind and quality of relationship that Jesus makes possible. For Paul, "grace" isn't something you say at mealtime; rather, it's the word that sums up all of what God has done to reconcile us to himself. So Paul will say, "by grace you have been saved" (Ephesians 2:5).

My son Spencer taught me that we're saved by grace *so we can be gracious to one another*. Grace is something we give, accepting others in their weakness. And graciousness is so important if we're going to raise up young leaders for God's movement in our day. So much of what the church calls "ministry" is really about making someone what we want them to be. We think leadership development is about telling younger people how we got to be the good Christians we are, and we don't want to affirm them until they become like us. So we're constantly disappointed and frustrated by their inability to be what we think they should be. This kind of self-righteousness can infect any movement that's really trying to make a difference in the world. It's poisonous. It stifles people and kills a movement.

I don't think we need to go around parading our righteousness. To tell the truth, I don't really want people to know that I'm a Christian until they discover it for themselves. Not long ago I was on an airplane reading my Bible. The businessman beside me wanted to know if I was a preacher, but he was too polite to just come out and ask. So he said, "What do you do?" I didn't want him to know I'm a Christian because he already knew what he thought of Christians. So I said, "I'm a developer. I help people develop their communities so that everyone can flourish." He was interested in that. We talked for a long time.

Paul doesn't tell Timothy what he needs to do in order to be as good as Paul. Instead, he tells him to be strong in grace. How can you be strong in grace? I think the more you receive it, the stronger you can be in giving it. We grow stronger in grace as we practice it in relationships. But you have to be in real relationship with people. You have to be there in the community. Sometimes I hear preachers say, "I love you, and God loves you too." But I don't believe they love me if they don't know me. You've got to know people if you're really going to communicate God's love to them.

Paul says "be strong in the grace that is in Christ Jesus. And the things you have heard me say in the presence of many witnesses entrust to reliable people who will also be qualified to teach others" (2 Timothy 2:1-2). That's indigenous leadership development as a model for God's movement in the world. We are invited into this movement through authentic relationships. That's how we know we're loved and it's how we learn to love. So we invite others to join God's movement through relationships, entrusting to them the good news that someone entrusted to us. This is how God has chosen to work in the world. Nothing is more important to God's movement than authentic relationships of grace from one generation to the next.

For years now I've had an early-morning Bible study at my breakfast table. That's where I do my leadership development. I do it early to weed out the ones who aren't really serious about it. If you're willing to get up for 5:30 a.m. Bible study, I know you're serious. So I invite the young guys to come and study the Bible with me. We read the Scriptures and we talk about how God wants to use us in society. That's what evangelism means for me. I'm entrusting to those young men what God has entrusted to me.

GOD CHOOSES TO WORK THROUGH US

I love the story about old farmer Ben out in the country who didn't care much for church. He kept to himself and raised beautiful crops, but Ben wasn't very religious. Religious people didn't sit well with him. An evangelist heard about old Ben and went out to see him. He walked through his fields and admired the produce. "Brother Ben," the evangelist said, even though he knew full well Ben wasn't a brother, "the Lord has certainly blessed you with a bountiful harvest on this good land." The evangelist's voice was pious and confident. He so wanted to convince Ben that he needed God. But Ben said, "You should have seen the place when the Lord had it to himself."

We religious people tend to lean on the supernatural. We always want God to prove himself with a sign. But God works through people. That's the incredible thing about grace. God doesn't only save us; he also works through us—redeemed sinners—to redeem the world. Even more incredible is the fact that God is sovereign and doesn't need us at all. But he *chooses* to work with us, to work through us. I don't know if we really understand grace until we grasp this idea that God chooses to need broken people like us in his plan to redeem the world.

This is why the church is so important. The church is where we are formed to become the beloved community God uses to do his will in society. The next great awakening that I see coming is a renewal of what it means to be church. For this generation of young people, church isn't going to be a social club where you gather once or twice a week to recharge your personal faith. It's not going to be an institution that wields its power in society either. The world is tired of Christian plans to fix things. It is starving for the kind of authentic relationships that Christ makes possible as we're reconciled to one another in his body, the church.

Authentic relationships in a reconciled community are giving young people confidence that they can do something in this world. That's what I see right here in my neighborhood. Young black men who have been held captive by their victim status are emerging as indigenous leaders for a new kind of church. Young white women who have been paralyzed by guilt are coming here and learning how God can use them to serve alongside others as change agents in society. In my later years, these are the signs of hope that keep me going.

I think of Ruth, a white woman who came here with a mission team when she was a student at Seattle Pacific University (SPU). She worked alongside people in our neighborhood. She came to my Bible studies and listened to people here, and got fired up about reconciliation. So she went back to her college and called the president's office. Ruth said she wanted the president of SPU to come to Jackson with the next group of students. The secretary in the office took all the information down, talked to the president and then called Ruth back. The president was glad to hear about the trip and wished that he could come, but he had other commitments, the secretary said.

But Ruth wouldn't take no for an answer. She got down to details and figured out how to make it work for the president to come down here with her. She told him she knew SPU could do something down here and that they should, so he had to come. And he did. He came down and we developed a partnership. Now there's a John Perkins Center for Reconciliation and Development at SPU. Students are coming down here and I'm going up there and we're working together to see what God can do through us. After Ruth graduated, she taught math in the Delta of Mississippi. Every once in a while, she would come up here on a weekend and visit with us. She's become part of our family.

Ruth gives me hope that a new generation of young people are ready to connect the gospel of reconciliation with their lives and make a real difference in society. She's not coming down here to "save the poor black children." She's facilitating real partnership and experiencing transformation in her own life as she becomes part of a new people—a beloved community that's much bigger and broader than the campus she came from.

But Ruth didn't leave her campus behind. She brought the whole community into partnership with our community, and we've all been changed in the process. New relationships are giving rise to new programs and institutions. And thousands of people are feeling the impact. It's starting to feel like we're really part of something big that God is doing in this generation.

Like with Ruth, I also get excited when I think about my grandson John. I love John so much, and he's always been a good kid. When he got to be a teenager we were asking John what he wanted to do, and he said he wanted to become an architect. So after high school, he was ready to go to college and study architecture. But that summer we had a young man whom we'd been working with come out of prison. He was living here in the neighborhood and got a good job working as a chef in a kitchen. That summer before John was supposed to go to college, this fellow helped John get a job working in the kitchen. And John loved it. He decided he didn't want to be an architect anymore. He wanted to be a chef. So he found the best culinary school around and got trained. Now he's back here in Jackson, running a kitchen for a big conference center.

John is a young black man with a good job. He's married to a wonderful woman, Patrice, and they have given me a great-grandson—John Philip Perkins. I'm so proud of John. But the thing that encourages me the most is how John has been coming to my early-morning Bible study these past few years. Next to his job and family, I think it's become the most important thing in his life. He doesn't miss it for anything. And he's been sharing with me his and Patrice's vision for a home church in the community.

Now, this gets me excited in my later years to watch my grandson imagining a new kind of church. He looks around our neighborhood and sees so many churches. But he knows these churches aren't connecting with the real needs in so many people's lives. The young men and women in our community aren't going to these churches. I've told John about the "house church" movement, but he says that won't work either. It's not going to work to just have a smaller replica of church as we know it meeting in living rooms. People need more than a place to gather to talk about their spiritual lives. They need a place where authentic relationship happens. They need a place where individuals and families can heal. They need little outposts of the beloved community where people share life and learn to follow Jesus together.

My grandson John is on the cutting-edge of something God is doing in this generation. I'm as excited as he is to get up for early-morning Bible study and see where God is taking us. Black people have been so wounded by racism that we can easily get trapped in our anger and pass on our damage rather than offering something new. We do this through the institutions that we've established—even the church. So much of our current church life is about reinforcing what we already know about who we are and what we think we can become. Jesus too easily becomes a sweet song to get us through in a world that never changes.

But John is right there on the edge of imagining something new. He's looking at the community with me and he's seeing how our institutional church has failed to invite people into authentic relationships of love. We haven't experienced reconciliation and the freedom Christ offers in that because we've focused so much on the negative—our victim status in a world that's done us wrong. John can see that we need to invite people into institutions of love where they know God in a new kind of relationship with brothers and sisters in Christ.

Among young white folks like Ruth and young black folks like John and so many others that I meet around the country, God is planting the seeds of the next great awakening. I can't imagine a more exciting time to be alive. I lived through the Civil Rights movement forty years ago, and we saw some exciting things then. It was exciting to be part of a movement where people were learning that they had dignity and could stand up on their own two feet. But the Civil Rights movement died on the brink of some real human development. We glimpsed the beloved community, but we also watched it slip away because the movement lost its foundation in God's greater movement.

That's why there's no time in history when I would rather be living than right now. The church has lost its position of power in society, but it almost seems like we're seeing firsthand what Christ meant when he said "my strength is made perfect in weakness." In our weakness the church is finding new forms for life together based on Jesus' model of discipleship and leadership development that invites people into the authentic relationships that reconciliation makes possible. The Civil Rights movement is over, and I'm not trying to make it come back. But God's movement continues, whether we get on board with it or not. My prayer for the institutional church is that we won't miss this opportunity to develop the church as the body of Christ and to equip the saints to really serve people and become the beloved community in society.

5

God's Movement in the Twenty-First Century

CHARLES MARSH

*J*ohn is right to be hopeful about a new generation. Despite popular characterizations of undergraduates as party-obsessed and jaded, there is a resurgence of moral energy in many of the universities of North America, and this resurgence is quite often fueled by religious convictions and inspired by many of the great social movements of the past.

Matthew and Amanda read Dorothy Day and Peter Maurin, and joined the Catholic Worker Movement. With their young son, they live in a community of Christian peacemakers in Maryhouse in New York City and give themselves to the homeless, exiled, hungry and forsaken. Like many students I've taught, Dylan and Lindsay read John's *Let Justice Roll Down*, visited Voice of Calvary in Mississippi on an "alternative spring break" and discerned the call of service. After graduation they moved into Charlottesville's Prospect neighborhood to work with children from low-income families. Studying the life and legacies of Dietrich Bonhoeffer, Mrs. Hamer and Dr. King inspired Charlene to use her prodigious intellectual gifts to encourage greater involvement of student ministries in justice and peacemaking. Lawson and Margaux came from privileged families and developed a heart for racial reconciliation as students at the university. In a prayer meeting after a hate crime on campus, they said, "It was only through the honesty enabled by prayer that this university can ever know anything about confession and forgiveness, and we can begin to reconcile." There are so many similar stories to tell. It's an exciting time to be a professor.

My courses on religion and progressive organizing fill to capacity with students eager to learn more about the theological and moral sources of social hope, community building and human rights. I say this not as a reflection on my own teaching— the older I get the more I feel that my job as a teacher is to offer some perspective and commentary, assign some great books, and then move to the side. I say it rather as a reflection on an emerging culture that came of age during years of war, deception and disillusionment, and that is now refusing to relinquish responsibility for the future to those people who presumed that the paradigm of war and greed was the only way to negotiate the harsh realities of the world.

A new generation of student leaders and activists gives us reason to hope that better days lie ahead. Young men and women inspired by the dream of beloved community spend spring breaks building houses in rural and urban areas and give their time to homeless shelters. They organize on behalf of undocumented workers and single mothers and abused children, form interracial and interfaith prayer groups, and develop networks of caring and compassion. They cook meals in hospitality houses, devote their Saturdays to block parties in low-income neighborhoods, volunteer in after-school tutorials, organize creatively for environmental care and fair distribution of national resources. Despite all the reasons to be cynical, many young people are saying, as the SNCC leader Diane Nash said more than four decades ago, "Our goal is to rehabilitate, to heal, to tap the energies of the soul, rather than to gain power or assert control."[1]

The resurgence of faith-based activism and community organization in recent decades is in some ways a rekindling of the Civil Rights movement's pursuit of redemptive community. At its best, this current movement (I like Clarence Jordan's phrase "the God movement") seeks to reclaim, and at times even to make explicit, the theological commitments that animated the Civil Rights movement. What's more, Christian community organizing puts these commitments to the test in building community among the poor and the excluded, and organizing for the poor. These intentional communities demonstrate the countercultural power of the gospel and teach us important lessons about the difference between the nation and the kingdom of God.

In recent years, the faith-based movement was seized by "compassionate conservatives" to exemplify the socially transformative power of religious institutions and to justify cuts in federal social spending. But that is not the end of the story. In fact, the faith-based movement in its most exuberant forms has roots in the Civil Rights movement and in many of America's most creative experiments in community building and organizing. At its best, this quiet revolution seeks to reclaim and renew the theological vision that animated the Civil Rights movement, putting the vision to work by building community among the poor and organizing for power.

Perhaps John Perkins's life and witness can serve as a prism to help distinguish the gifts that a theological imagination offer at the beginning of the twenty-first century. While I certainly cannot exhaust the range of issues illuminated by Perkins's quiet revolution, I do want to name three interlocking gifts that seem central: a deeper ecclesiology, a contemplative stillness and a bolder humility for the sake of the flourishing of humanity. Inasmuch as Perkins helps us see these gifts more clearly, he invites us into a space where we may celebrate that God has not left us without hope.

LIVING INTO A NEW CITIZENSHIP

What has become of the God movement that broke through in the Civil Rights movement onto ordinary streets of ordinary towns? Those with eyes to see can say that it is alive and well, always there to remind the church of what we are called to be.

I am encouraged by the hunger among a new generation for a deeper ecclesiology—and for a richer understanding of what it means to be the church in the world.

The earliest writings of the Christian tradition gave voice to the transnational identity of the faith community. In one of his most widely quoted meditations on the new identity of the Christian, the apostle Paul wrote that "all of you who were baptized into Christ have clothed yourselves with Christ," and there is now "neither Jew nor Gentile, neither slave nor free, neither male nor female, for you are all one in Christ Jesus" (Galatians 3:27-28). Paul's explorations of life "in Christ" amplify the theme of the "new creation" and the new being's capacity to cross boundaries and to reshape loyalties. Baptism is the sacrament that brings the person into the body of Christ, which is, among other things, an alternative social world, the new humanity. "For we were all baptized by one Spirit so as to form one body—whether Jews or Gentiles, slave or free—and we were all given the one Spirit to drink" (1 Corinthians 12:13).

As an institution with diminishing social influence in the West, the Protestant church in the nineteenth and twentieth centuries too often strove to make itself relevant to a world that was not sure it needed God. This led church leaders to deemphasize the peculiar and the secret in Christian life. Today, however, we hear voices calling us as a global, ecumenical church to retrieve the distinctive resources of the Christian theological tradition. In recent decades, the center of gravity in the Christian world has shifted dramatically southward to Asia, Latin America and

Africa. The largest Christian communities in the world today are found in Africa and Latin America, and the trend points toward a global majority of nonwhite, non-Western Christians within a few decades.[2]

My friend Mark Gornik is a minister in the Christian Reformed Church and dean of City Seminary in Harlem. Aside from his duties in academic administration and pastoral ministry, Mark has invested considerable time in studying the rise of immigrant churches in the five boroughs of New York. The title of his recent doctoral dissertation, "The Word Made Global," captures his perspective on the shifting patterns of world Christianity. The *New York Times* featured Mark's research on world Christianity and globalization in a front-page Sunday feature story titled "Where the Gospel Resounds in African Tongues."[3]

In an effort to understand the story of the revival of churches on the margins, which he calls "globalization from below," Mark has counted more than two hundred new African churches in New York City alone. As he sees it, the lessons of the story of world Christianity are essential for evangelical and mainline congregations in the United States.

The African immigrant churches in New York, like all churches affected by the crosscultural diffusion of the gospel, follow the plot line of the Acts of the Apostles, the action-packed New Testament narrative of the earliest Christian communities. The plot is that of the church quickly becoming multicultural in the first generation, attracting diverse people to Jesus who worship together in ever more culturally inclusive forms. Importantly, neither in the early Christian churches nor in New York today is religious transformation a result of top-down decisions by elites; transformation results "from grassroots movements and the initiative of people from around the world."[4] Mark sees the globalization from below, both in the flourishing immigrant congregations in New York (and throughout the United States) and in the rise of global Christianity.

On a summer afternoon in Harlem, Mark explained to me that the stories of new immigrant communities in the urban centers of the West can help remind American Christians of the basic purpose of the church in the world. "Christians in the United States are not at the center of the Christian world," Mark says. "The global Christian movement is not the American story, as difficult as that might be for us to hear."[5] He feels that believers in North America urgently need to grasp this reality—that the center of gravity in global Christianity is fast shifting from the North to the Global South—as well as the significance of the monumental changes in the new religious landscape.

These new Christians in the southern hemisphere, with their intense spiritual energies for holiness and mission, are God's reminder that the kingdom of God is a world movement. While we often act as if our mission is to build and fortify clusters of like-minded believers, the immigrant churches call us to live in the world as pilgrim people. "The problem with white evangelicals in the U.S. is that we so often do not get outside of our own culture," Mark says. "We are incomplete as Christians if we are culturally isolated. We are not the people we should be." Growing in the faith and living with a greater mindfulness of the kingdom means reckoning ever more fully with the new shape of the church.

Mark calls the rise of immigrant churches in New York "an Ephesians moment." To illustrate the point, he offers the "subway test" as evidence. Whenever he rides the subway, Mark likes to look around the car to see who is reading the Bible. New York City is sometimes regarded as a great secular metropolis, but Mark finds signs of renewal in the ordinary and sometimes forgotten places of the city. On subway cars in Harlem he sees men and women, teenagers and children, reading Scripture or devotional books. Sometimes they are standing with one hand on the rail and the other clutching a pocket-size New Testament. Usually these people are African or Hispanic, or from other new immigrant communities in the city.

As we walked back along Frederick Douglass Boulevard toward City Seminary, Mark offered an insight from his research that might well be claimed as the basis of all preaching and evangelism in the ecumenical church. "The diaspora is the mission," he said. "Learning to live as though 'diaspora' itself were the mission fundamentally changes the way we think about the Christian life."

It is not surprising to hear that Pastor Gornik, after finishing seminary twenty years ago, was mentored by John Perkins at Voice of Calvary and has sought to implement the vision he learned there in the urban landscapes of the northeastern cities.

CONTEMPLATION AND CHRIST

In an increasingly post-Christian society, many of our wisest pastors and teachers keep saying that we must learn to live as keepers of the mystery. We don't need to shout the gospel louder than competing messages so much as we need to learn to be quiet in a noisy nation. Quietness and stillness must nourish our actions, words and songs.

"Teaching about Christ begins in silence," Bonhoeffer told the students in his 1933 lectures on the doctrine of Christ. "The silence of the church is the silence before the Word."[6] The man or woman in Christ lives in reference to a new center. Christian thinking and acting emerge from encounter with Jesus Christ, which brings the crusading ego to stillness before the Word.

"You are fed up with words," Thomas Merton said, two decades after Bonhoeffer's death, "and I don't blame you. I am nauseated by them sometimes. I am also, to tell the truth, nauseated by ideals and with causes. This sounds like heresy, but I think you will understand what I mean."[7] In fact, I don't think this sounds like heresy at all. It sounds like the honest observations of a Christian who has grown tired of all the trivial spiritual talk.

The philosopher Max Picard wrote in his meditations on solitude, "In the modern world the individual no longer faces silence, no longer faces the community, but faces only the universal noise."[8] Sometimes it seems as if we prefer the noise. I can say for sure that this is the case for me. The noise feels comforting; the noise shields us from difficult and demanding truths.

But the Scriptures teach us a different lesson.

"Be still, and know that I am God," the psalmist says (46:10). The psalmist! Be still and *know*.

The psalm offers us an invitation to learn again who we are as children of the living God, to live in thanksgiving for God's love, to stand in worshiping stillness in God's presence, to behold God's resplendent beauty and alien peace, putting aside the relentless production of programs and projects and our grand self-estimations, and to live in what Merton called "Evangelical Joy."

I am encouraged by those who are turning to the contemplative—the monastic, even—in the West today. For the past decade, "new monastic" communities have been springing up in urban centers and on the forgotten farmlands of the North American landscape. Filled with young people who are passionate about injustice and eager for change, these communities are also attuned to God's peculiar way of bringing about change in the world. They have decided that prayer is more radical than protest, and that the vocation of contemplatives in community is to "become the answer to our prayers."[9]

The disciplines of prayer and contemplative stillness make space for the remembrance of who we are in Christ. The second-century theologian Irenaeus of Lyons described the redemptive death of Jesus Christ as the hidden center of all being, the sum of the world's known and unknown longings, which recapitulates the whole of estranged and broken creation to its original purpose. The incarnation revivifies the deep structures of the created order so that all creation and all its glorious diversity are gathered together and embraced in Christ. The real history of the world is revealed in the story of Jesus.

Irenaeus explained in his treatise *Against Heresies,* "[As] in super-celestial, spiritual and invisible things, the Word is Supreme, so also in things visible and corporeal He might possess the supremacy, and taking to Himself the preeminence, as well as constituting Himself Head of the Church, He might draw all things to Himself at the proper time."[10] Jesus Christ redeemed, reconstructed and reconstituted the created order which, until the coming of God in the flesh, had been subjected to final obliteration, estranged from its Source, advancing in a slow but certain march into nonbeing. But the incarnation of God in Jesus Christ is the advent of perfect peace, which Christians believe to be the real meaning of life—life more abundant.

These are sublime and ponderous notions, the story of the whole architecture of being crumbling beneath the weight of human rebellion yet redeemed now in the coming of Christ. But it is also a conception which, once grasped, inspires the mind toward a joyful but sober apprehension of reality: Christ representing in word and truth the first Adam, rescuing in himself "all the dispersed peoples dating back to Adam, all tongues and the whole race of mankind, along with Adam himself," "recapitulating in Himself the long sequence of mankind."[11]

This means that now, in the time after the great events of the cross and resurrection, we see all things in a new light. Celebrating life with God, we accept the good news that Jesus has taken the place of our judgment, suffered on the cross for the disobedience of Adam and born the punishment which we deserve, gathering up all humanity into the fellowship of the Father, Son and Holy Spirit.

In a letter from Tegel prison, where he spent the final years of his life before being executed by the Gestapo in 1945, German theologian Dietrich Bonhoeffer recalled Irenaeus's idea as a "magnificent conception," "full of comfort." "Everything is taken up in Christ," Bonhoeffer said, "although it is transformed."[12] Irenaeus's account of the ontological rebirth of the world in Christ brings relief and consolation. We learn that the Christian's primary mission is to learn to be participants in God's good and glorious creation. We are relieved of the burden of re-creating the world in our own image and the exhausting task of seeking to orchestrate God's will. Christ and Christ alone "give[s] [the world] back to us," Bonhoeffer says, as a gift.

What does this ancient Christian formulation have to do with God's movement and the church's vocation in our time? I can imagine Irenaeus, in the company of the church fathers and mothers, the saints and the martyrs, and all the faithful stewards of Christian truth over our two-thousand-year history, asking with John Perkins, What does it mean to the body of Christ and "to equip the saints with the gifts of the Spirit for real service to real people"?[13]

A BOLDER HUMILITY

In his book *Ethics,* Dietrich Bonhoeffer makes a remark that I find as provocative and arresting as any other passage in his writings.

Bonhoeffer, a theologian and martyr who helped form a dissenting church in Nazi Germany, wrote a trenchant account of Christian discipleship, titled *The Cost of Discipleship,* that includes the line "When Jesus calls a person to follow, he bids that person come and die."[14] Bonhoeffer was a theologian of deliberate and disciplined piety, who grieved over the collapse of the church and sang the Negro spirituals with his fellow German dissidents.

But in *Ethics,* the complexity of the age (much like our own time) marked a change in the theological and moral nature of Christian witness in the world. Bonhoeffer says, "In earlier times the church could preach that a person must first become a sinner, like the publican and the harlot, before he could know and find Christ, but we in our time must say rather that before a person can know and find Christ he must first become righteous like those who strive and who suffer for the sake of justice, truth and humanity."[15]

What does this mean? Bonhoeffer was not giving up on Christ and embracing secular humanism. On the contrary, he was moving more fully into the depth and richness of discipleship to Christ. Part of that discipleship is seeing, as Brother Merton urged us to see, that our calling as Christians does not make us superior to other people. Those who come to the work of mercy and justice from places outside the church are drawn by a power which the church eloquently articulates, but which it should not seek to control. We are not called to be masters of the truth, as if truth were our possession. Instead, the church's recognition of "good people" should chasten Christian ambitions to impose the church's language on every human conflict and situation of need.

Nor should the church be envious of those who come to justice by other names either. Rather, we need to listen to them, learn lessons from them, and demonstrate a willingness to link arms with all those who care about the human condition and the created order. We might be humbled by and grateful for the opportunity to participate in a common human struggle for a just world. Our job as Christians is "to struggle along with everybody else and collaborate with them in the difficult, frustrating task of seeking a solution to common problems, which are entirely new and strange to us all."[16]

This illuminates both our hope and our discipline: to speak with the humility required by our fallible vision and by speaking to take part in the shared human struggle. "One must not only preach a sermon with his voice," Martin Luther King Jr. said, "he must preach it with his life."[17] Let us, abiding with Christ, pray that we may learn to relinquish our claims on God and to see that shared struggle is the place where proper humility is forever nourished.

A theological lesson of the Civil Rights movement offers us a good way to think of the shape of our hope: The beloved community is the new social space inaugurated by the great event of the cross where all people are invited to partake in the welcoming table of God. Here we share common cause in a common struggle. Here we borrow each hope from our brothers and sisters and children for a better future. Here we work for mercy and justice in what Dr. King called "the fierce urgency of now." Here we learn to dwell in the radiant peace of Christ.

To build such beloved community with all people was the

driving vision of the movement that grew out of King's encounter with the living Christ and Fannie Lou Hamer's welcoming table. A Christian vision for beloved community does not exclude the stranger but rather welcomes them into the peace that God makes possible—a peace that God may well have already given them some insight into. "These things I have spoken to you," Jesus says in the sixteenth chapter of St. John's Gospel, "that in Me you may have peace. In the world you will have tribulation; but be of good cheer, I have overcome the world" (NKJV). There is no greater gift we could offer our neighbors than to live as a people who have peace in a world so broken by violence.

AFTER THE MOVEMENT DIES
Voice of Calvary and the Spencer Perkins Center have not fixed West Jackson. The surrounding neighborhood is still one of the most violent in the nation today. But on weeknights, John Perkins can often be found at the Perkins Center talking to a group of student volunteers. He leads Bible studies and presents the "three Rs" model for community development with as much enthusiasm as he did forty years ago, when his family went from Mendenhall to the capital city. The SNCC volunteers of Freedom Summer have long since left Mississippi, moved on to other things and left the unfinished business to local people. But John and Vera Mae Perkins, along with their children, grandchildren, and a diverse extended family of brothers and sisters in Christ, have stayed.

"The civil rights movement died on the brink of some real human development," John Perkins has said. "We must have some people who will keep moving after the movement dies, after it is no longer popular to do what is right."[18] The Civil Rights movement may have moved on, but God's movement continues in the world. Witnesses like John and Vera Mae Perkins remind us of the kind of lives God can still make possible. Young people who are eager to sing more beautiful songs—and who find the church in sometimes unfamiliar and unexpected places—give us hope that we are on the brink of something new. For so long Christian language has been hijacked by peddlers of prosperity gospel and nationalistic religion. But as Christendom loses its handle on the reins of power in Western culture, perhaps God is giving us pause to remember who we are in Christ.

If this is a season of relative quietness into which we have entered, then may we take the time to remember that thinking and acting marked by the sign of the cross bring the crusading ego and our messianic ambitions to a humble and listening stillness. May we heed the wisdom of the Eucharistic hymn, a hymn that comes to Christians from the book of Zechariah in the Hebrew Bible, "Let all mortal flesh keep silence."

But may our silence also teach us that though we are to be slow to speak, we are also called to proclaim a distinctive word and live a distinctive life in the world.

Let me tell you one more story before John brings the book to a close in his final chapter. One of the greatest joys of the years I have spent studying the Civil Rights movement has been my friendship with the late Victoria Gray Adams, whom I mentioned earlier. Mrs. Adams was a church lady and business leader of Hattiesburg, Mississippi, who became a field secretary for the SNCC and a sister traveler with Fannie Lou Hamer. After the movement years she settled in Petersburg, Virginia, with her husband and family. She served as the Wesleyan chaplain at Virginia State University.

Shortly before she died in 2006, Mrs. Adams visited one of my undergraduate seminars at the University of Virginia. We were meeting in my home that afternoon. It was a cold winter day, and we gathered our chairs around the fireplace, listening to this riveting storyteller and civil rights saint. There was a wonderful spirit in the room. Mrs. Adams had a gift for invoking the spirit of the movement in a way that was palpable, and soon we were all singing freedom songs and spirituals. In what proved to be our last conversation, Victoria Gray Adams was asked by a student, "What is the mission of the Civil Rights movement today?" Without hesitation she said, "It is learning to speak the language of peace."[19]

Mrs. Adams gave voice to the most urgent need of our age. Certainly the practice of peace and learning to speak the language of peace includes a wide range of social practices, but her answer would be the first response I would give to the question Where do we go from here?

Maybe the greatest gift John Perkins has to offer us is a learning program in the language of peace. My favorite picture of John is the one that graces the cover of his book *A Quiet Revolution*. On the porch of a sharecropper's shack in rural Mississippi, John is sitting on the edge of a wooden chair, leaning into a conversation with a white-haired woman in a rocking chair. His eyes are attentive, and he is listening. "Living involvement," John has said, "turns poor people from statistics into friends." And friendship across the dividing lines of our society may be the best chance we have of relearning the language of peace. From Irenaeus to Dietrich Bonhoeffer, Christian theology reminds us that such friendship is possible because God has crossed every barrier to become friends with us. The lived theology of John Perkins's witness makes palpable the Word of peace which is made flesh in the new humanity of Jesus Christ.

As a corrective to the often self-indulgent pieties of American Christendom, John Perkins has shown in word and deed that Christian discipleship requires people to reevaluate their personal desires, prejudices, opinions and economic policies in the light of God's moral demands. He has called Christians in North America to be known far and wide as people with "a burden for the poor and oppressed," who "plead the case of the poor, defending the weak, helping the helpless." The gospel comes to us from a country far from our own. In this way, Perkins shows us that to read the Bible faithfully is to read the Bible as the *comprehensive divine plan of human liberation from the perspective of God's peaceable kingdom.* While this plan can never be identified with one political party or ideology, it undoubtedly requires some degree of public advocacy for economic policies preferential to the poor and oppressed. The habits and practices that sustain beloved community are the gifts of the church, broken and fallible, and yet still the one enduring source of forgiveness and reconciliation in our bruised and violent world.

6

A Time for Rebuilding

JOHN M. PERKINS

The problems of my community are the problems of America. I've lived and ministered in poor communities for fifty years now, and I can tell you that the issue we're facing is the broken family and the broken community. It really is a single issue. The community is broken because families are broken, and families can't get back together because the community is broken. This is why family values and social justice aren't separate issues. The health of the community depends on the health of the family and the health of the family depends on the justice of the community. If the church is going to offer good news in our time, we have to give some alternative to the broken family and broken community that reflect the desperation of our culture.

Injustice in our society has broken up the black family from slavery up until today. That's what the blues was all about. In the 1920s when black women started going north to Chicago and Gary, Indiana, to take domestic jobs, men in Mississippi started singing, "My baby's gone . . . and I'll be going too." But they couldn't go. There weren't jobs for them. So they stayed on the farms as sharecroppers, working behind someone else's plow to pay a debt they could never get out from under. Pretty soon they found another woman. And their wives up north started having other men's babies. The family was broken up by economic injustice. And the community suffered as people with access to resources got out and those who couldn't leave got desperate.

Our churches have done little more than reproduce and radiate this brokenness of our culture. Where the church has grown in numbers over the past generation, it has been captivated by the "homogenous unit principle." This church-growth strategy says people are more likely to come to a church where most of the other people are like them. So pastors in the suburbs catered their services and programs to middle-class "seekers." And they built big churches of middle-class people. Short-term mission trips became the main connection between these churches and poor people. Which means the poor aren't members of our big churches. They're out there somewhere, in need of help. A whole lot of our churches have decided to outsource justice.

If the gospel of reconciliation is going to interrupt the brokenness in society, our churches are going to have to rethink their vocation. When I read the Bible, I always bring the problems of my community to God and ask when in history God's people have had to face a similar challenge. God is the same yesterday, today and forever. But God also chooses to walk with his people in history. That means we can't know the will of God for us today unless we're paying attention to what's happening and how God wants to work in this situation. As I look at our situation today and the problems we face, I hear God speaking to the church in the words that he spoke through his prophets after the exile. Coming out of our cultural captivity, I hear God saying that this is a time for rebuilding the church and remembering what it really means to be Christ's body in the world.

ZECHARIAH'S VISION OF A PEACEFUL CITY

After God's people had been scattered all over the world, they came back to their land to reestablish themselves in Zion. They came back ready to rebuild their society. But the prophets said God's people had the world in them. They forgot God and his temple in Jerusalem. Their only motivation was greed. They had the culture of the world in them and it kept them from serving God. So the prophets after the exile wrote about what God was going to do to save his people after they'd become captive to the world's culture. I love to read these prophets. Even though they can sound harsh, I hear them speaking to the problems of our time. They speak to the broken family and the broken community. And they reveal that God has a plan to fix all our brokenness.

Of all the prophets who wrote after the exile, Zechariah is my favorite. He understands the problems of my neighborhood. And he says God's going to fix this mess we're in. All I have to do is join up and be part of what God is already doing: "This is what the LORD says: 'I will return to Zion and dwell in Jerusalem. Then Jerusalem will be called the City of Truth, and the mountain of the LORD Almighty will be called the Holy Mountain. . . . Once again men and women of ripe old age will sit in the streets of Jerusalem, each of them with cane in hand because of their age. The city streets will be filled with boys and girls playing there'" (Zechariah 8:3-5).

God knows that the very old and the very young are the most vulnerable in our society. That's who God is concerned about. We've got to take care of the old people because they have the wisdom to pass on to the boys and girls. In God's vision of a just and peaceful city, the old folks sit in the streets with their canes in their hands and the children play around them. This is how human society was made to work, and God says he's going to make it happen.

Zechariah understands the economics of broken communities. "People could not go about their business safely because of conflicts," the Lord says, "since I had turned them all against each other" (Zechariah 8:10). When people are out of work and poor, the one who doesn't have is going to steal from the one who does. We know that. God knows it too. So God promises not to punish his people anymore, but to bless them: "The seed will grow well, the vine will yield its fruit, the ground will produce its crops, and the heavens will drop their dew" (Zechariah 8:12). Everyone is working in this city, and God is providing his part. The people till the soil, God provides the rain, and the harvest is bountiful. There is no welfare line. Families are together and the community is peaceful because everyone has a good job. When people are working and God is giving the increase, the community is at peace.

I was driving in a cold rain not long ago, and when I stopped for a red light, I looked out and saw a man standing on the street corner, begging for money. He was a healthy man—healthier than me. If I stood out in the rain like that at my age, I'd be in bed for a week. But there he was just standing in the rain, without any work to do. A community where men stand in the rain to beg is broken. There is no peace in that city. It's that man's problem, but it's also our community's problem. We've got to do something to make good work possible for healthy people like him.

What does the church have to offer a community where healthy men beg on the street corner? God wanted Israel to be a blessing to the nations, but they became captive to the world's culture. They lived like everybody else. They didn't bless the nations with God's good way of living. They were a curse, and they became the object of other people's greed and selfishness. But in Zechariah, this is what the Lord says: "I will give all these things as an inheritance to the remnant of this people. Just as you, Judah and Israel, have been a curse among the nations, so I will save you, and you will be a blessing" (8:12-13).

God wants to make us a blessing in the midst of our broken society. He doesn't need a big crowd of people. A remnant is enough. We don't have to worry about being too small or too weak. If we do our part, God promises to do his. We till the soil; God gives the rain. If we are faithful, God will be faithful, and we will become a blessing to the nations. Here's what we've got to do, Zechariah says: "Speak the truth to each other, and render true and sound judgment in your courts; do not plot evil against each other, and do not love to swear falsely" (8:16-17).

God's people have to offer some kind of alternative to the brokenness around us in the world. Zechariah shows us that our courts and prison system reflect the brokenness of society. Mississippi is about as wicked as you can get. Over the years I've become aware that the lawyers run Mississippi. The business people don't run our state; the lawyers do. They will sue anybody. They put up their money to elect the judges, and these days there's a story in the paper almost every week about how a lawyer used his money to bribe a judge in some case. Our courts and our jails reflect society's wickedness.

God never wanted jails. Prison is a reflection of our fallen society, and it is the responsibility of everyone to redeem our failure to be salt and light to these broken people. In Matthew 25 Jesus instructs us to visit the prisoner and says that on judgment day, he'll ask if we did. The church is called to be a blessing in places of brokenness, so God sends us to the jails. God wants us to interrupt this broken system with his love.

When we live out some alternative—when we show the world that there's a better way by how we live our lives in society—then our worship will become a celebration, Zechariah says: "The fasts of the fourth, fifth, seventh and tenth months will become joyful and glad occasions and happy festivals for Judah" (8:19). How could fasting be a celebration? The world is so greedy that it thinks the only way to enjoy life is to have more and more stuff. But God's people get together and go without food and stuff to celebrate God's goodness. I love that song that says, "The more we get together . . . the happier we will be." That's what life in beloved community is about. We get together and celebrate the goodness of our God that is better than all the stuff this world offers.

This prosperity gospel that has infected our poor neighborhoods is so poisonous because it lies about how God wants to bless us. God's blessings don't come out of the moon. They come when we till the soil and plant a seed. I look at these prosperity preachers on TV, and I see our poor black women falling out in front of them. Those women have been dehumanized by society, and they are so desperate for affirmation that they will give their last dollar to come in and testify on these preachers' shows. They let the women shout and feel good, and then they take a little money from them. These prosperity preachers call it "sowing a seed" when those women give their last dollar. But that's not sowing a seed. That's exploitation.

God says if we'll do our work, tell the truth and treat each other right, he will do his part and bless us. That's how God wants to bless us. It's not magic. If we plant and do our work, God will water and do his work. If we work hard to reflect the kingdom with our lives, Zechariah says that God is going to do the evangelism: "Many peoples and the inhabitants of many cities will yet come, and the inhabitants of one city will go to another and say, 'Let us go at once to entreat the Lord and seek the Lord Almighty. I myself am going'" (8:20-21). God wants to bless every nation, and he will do it. But our job is to be faithful in following God's way. We don't have to do any great works. God has already done the great work. We just need to get on board and become the community he's called us to be.

Making Beloved Community Happen

So what does it take to make beloved community happen? I really believe that it begins with a place. I've preached relocation all my life because the communities I've been part of have been abandoned. Everybody left, so I called them to come back. But my real concern is for the place. If the church is going to offer some real good news in broken communities, it has to be committed to a place. We can't just be a commuter church in the community.

In our community in West Jackson, we've got one of those churches where people drive in from all over town on Sunday morning. That church is not an asset to the community. Almost none of the congregation is from our community. It's a liability. All those cars jam up our streets on Sunday morning and make it hard for us to get around. And they do almost nothing to help the community. A church that wants to be about God's movement has to be committed to making a good life possible for people in the place where we are.

If you care about a place, you'll care about the kids in that place. If you don't care about the kids, they'll knock out your windows. But the kids in our neighborhood don't knock out our windows. One of the first things we did when we came here was to put in a sandbox and build a jungle gym. We made sure there was a field for the kids to play ball in. So now we can say, "Don't throw rocks. Go throw the ball in the field." The kids need to be able to play in the community, just like Zechariah says.

When you're committed to a place, you also care about the beauty of the place. The flowers around our place are important. Every summer the children come running to ask me if they can take some flowers home with them. They don't have pretty flowers at home. So I always tell them, "Yes, but wait till the end of the day. When you're going home you can cut a few and take them home to your mother." Shared beauty makes people want to share life together. You don't have to tend your flowers in a neighborhood very long before you have something to talk to your neighbors about.

It may sound simple, but I think you've got to have neighbors you talk to and get to know before you can love your neighbor as yourself. That's why community development has been so important to me all these years. The church can't organize the perfect community. If people aren't drawn by the cords of love to a vision of beloved community, you can't force it on them. But we can organize for justice. We can develop a community so that there is a place for people to know one another. That's the work God has given us to do. Only God can send the rain, but we can till the ground by committing to a place and making sure people can flourish there. That's the first thing the church has to do if we're going to interrupt the brokenness of society.

As we commit to our communities, we also need to learn how to see them as economic places. It's not enough to just move into a place, plant some flowers and be nice to your neighbors. All of that is good, but that won't address the brokenness of people's lives because the structures of the community are broken. People need work, good housing, education and health care. So the church has to invest its resources in developing the community. We also need to use our influence to get businesses and government to invest in the community. All of this is crucial to creating the conditions that are necessary for beloved community.

I'm fascinated by the way many Chinese immigrants build their communities around common work. In Mississippi many immigrants go into the restaurant business. They move to a place and open a restaurant, and everybody has a job. They're a tight-knit community. The Chinese have a strong community because they don't just spread out and get whatever work they can, each man for himself. They recognize the importance of working together.

I wish churches spent more time thinking about how their members could love one another and share a common life by working together as a community. Part of the reason our churches are so individualistic is that we just accept the economic system of our culture without question. We assume that the people who can get the good jobs should go wherever they have to and the people who can't get the good jobs should just take what they can get. But churches that want to interrupt the brokenness of society ought to be about creating jobs in the community and giving neighbors an opportunity to work together. If we take our communities seriously as economic places, we'll spend more time thinking about creating good work than we spend thinking about more relevant worship styles or bigger church buildings.

FORMING PEOPLE FOR GOD'S MOVEMENT

Community development is important, but it means very little if we're not also invested in the development of people. If you give people access to resources and education but don't form them for discipleship, then you're just setting them free from poverty to become slaves to individualism. This is what our so-called privileged churches are learning right now. They're learning that middle-class success isn't satisfying. People want more. They want meaning and connection. People want community, but they're not finding it in their lonely struggle to get a good job, a good house and a good retirement plan. The children of these families are coming home from college and telling mommy and daddy, "I want more than success."

I'm really encouraged by what I see happening in many churches around the nation. Take for example University Presbyterian Church in Seattle, Washington. University Presbyterian is an older church that has had a series of good pastors, and the church has done very well. But this church is in touch with the yearning of young people for community. A number of years ago a successful businessman who lived out on the islands decided to move back into the neighborhood where the church is located and start a discipleship program for young people. Some of his wealthy friends joined him, and now they have a number of houses right around the church where young people can live in a community of discipleship. They're a wealthy church, but they're investing their wealth in people, and they're forming those people to serve God's movement in Seattle and around the world.

If people are going to choose community and have the inner strength to sustain it in the face of broken families and broken communities, the church is going to have to form young people in habits and practices that are peculiar to the world around us. I think the Mennonites have done better than anyone else in America at instilling some restraint in their children. The Mennonites aren't poor. They own their farms, and their businesses make money. But they've developed a culture of asking, How much is enough? They've taught their children some restraint. They don't need the newest jeans or the nicest cars to believe that they have dignity or to enjoy God's good creation.

When we come into the kingdom of God, Jesus checks our values at the door. Our love for the stuff we have and our desires for stuff that we don't have—all of that gets called into question by God's movement. Will it help build the kingdom? Will it contribute to the beloved community? If not, we don't need it. It's getting in the way. I believe a rich man can get into heaven, but he's got to be converted. And it's not easy. So we've got to form people in a way of conversion. We've got to help our young people know how to constantly turn back to God, even when they have access to power and money and the things this world offers.

We've got to get over this idea that we're converted once and then we're through. Jesus said "Follow me" to Peter, and Peter followed. But Peter wasn't finished. He had some things to learn. Peter was the first to confess Jesus as Messiah, but Jesus also called him Satan, as we read only a few verses later in the Gospel narrative. Peter walked on the water, but he sank when he stopped trusting Jesus. Peter followed Jesus, but he also denied his Lord. He fell down more than once. But Peter learned that God wanted to help him get up again. That's what grace is all about. I think that's why Peter could write, "Make every effort to add to your faith goodness; and to goodness, knowledge; and to knowledge, self-control; and to self-control, perseverance; and to perseverance, godliness; and to godliness, mutual affection; and to mutual affection, love" (2 Peter 1:5-7). We grow in grace as we walk with Jesus, and that is what formation is all about—giving people grace so they can grow up into all that God wants them to be.

We won't have community until we develop people's character. Conversion and discipleship go hand in hand. They are the tools God uses to shape our character so that we become living members of a body that is inhabited and controlled by the Holy Spirit. These days I'm often asked to talk about the Civil Rights movement and what it meant to me. Almost always I talk about King's "I Have a Dream." I remember listening to his vision and hoping and praying that it could be true for my children. I have lived to see America elect its first black president, and what a happy day that was. We've made some progress toward not judging people by the color of their skin. But in our struggle to ensure civil rights for everyone, we can't forget the content of our character in society. We can't forget how important it is to shape character. If people are able to see beyond skin color, what is there for them to see? Character is formed in community, and community cannot be sustained without it.

This is why I'm so encouraged by my grandson John and his vision for a home church. That sounds to me like the kind of place where real formation could happen. In our neighborhood we know that the family is broken and the community is broken. What that really means is that each of us is broken. We need a place to be healed by God's grace. We need a place where we learn to be together—where we develop the skills and the patience that it will take to give one another grace. We can't make that happen. But we know that's what God wants to happen. And we know that he's going to do it. The good news is that we can be part of it now.

Indeed, the good news is that John is not the only young person in the church today who is searching for a way of life that makes beloved community possible for everyone. We're not there yet, but we are living in a new time. This is a time for rebuilding. I pray that every Christian, young and old alike, would have the courage to give themselves fully to God's movement toward reconciliation and the beloved community in society.

Study Guide

Questions for Personal Reflection or Group Discussion

CHAPTER 1: THE UNFINISHED BUSINESS OF THE CIVIL RIGHTS MOVEMENT

1. Charles describes Dr. Martin Luther King Jr.'s journey into the Civil Rights movement as somewhat unintentional, even reluctant. How has God been prodding you along in this journey toward community and reconciliation? What situations have you stumbled into that have opened your eyes to the injustice around you?

2. What does "beloved community" mean to Dr. King, Charles Marsh and John Perkins? What does it mean to you?

3. On pages 18-20 Charles talks about his life. How does his life experience affect his theology? What might be some ways that your life story and social location affect the way you think about God?

4. What did the church offer the Civil Rights movement?

5. What does it mean for America to be "ontologically evil" (p. 25)? How does that belief cripple social action?

6. What are the three Rs? How can you imagine living them out in your life? What in the three Rs can you least imagine yourself doing, and why?

7. Why does John Perkins say that "a people transformed and mobilized by Jesus Christ in their institutional behavior will consistently support economic policies preferential to the poor" (pp. 32-33)? How does that rub against the way we do business in the United States?

8. Charles writes, "Discipleship to Jesus Christ requires us to reevaluate our political preferences, personal desires, prejudices, opinions and economic policies in the light of God's moral demands" (p. 34). What did this chapter cause you to reevaluate?

CHAPTER 2: THE CULTURAL CAPTIVITY OF THE CHURCH

1. What are the public wounds of the black church? What are the hidden wounds of the white church? How have you seen them in your own life and community?

2. What is the nature of true human dignity? Why is it important?

3. How have you seen God interrupting the status quo? How has the church joined in Jesus' work of driving a wedge in the status quo? How has the church in your area upheld business as usual?

4. What kind of commitment does your church ask of you? What kind of commitment does John Perkins think God requires?

5. What does it mean to "make reconciliation a discipleship issue" (p. 51)?

6. Where do you see signs of God's movement in your community? How might you be called to join in? What do you risk in joining?

CHAPTER 3: THE POWER OF TRUE CONVERSION

1. Charles takes time in this chapter to tell some of the stories that have captured his heart and imagination. How do his stories capture your imagination? What are the stories that have drawn you into God's work of reconciliation?

2. What was the significance of John's gift of blueberries to Charles and his grandmother?

3. What did Charles learn from Fannie Lou Hamer? What can we learn?

4. Charles writes, "The existence of a compelling Christian witness in our time does not depend on our access to the White House, the size of our churches or the cultural relevance of our pastors. It depends, instead, on our ability to sing better songs with our lives" (p. 70). What does this mean?

5. How would you summarize the "song" that John Perkins and Fannie Lou Hamer are singing? How can you imagine joining in the song? Where specifically do you need God's grace in order to join in?

CHAPTER 4: THE NEXT GREAT AWAKENING

1. John suggests that this generation is longing for authentic relationships. How have you felt that need? How have you seen that need in your church or community?

2. John explains that Jesus' ministry was about loving a handful of people well. How is that description different than what you normally think of as Jesus' work? Do you agree with John that loving people well should be "our main plan for sharing the gospel" (p. 77)? Why is this a difficult vision to enact?

3. On page 80, John asks, "How can you be strong in grace?" What does the phrase "strong in grace" mean? How does John answer his own question? How would you answer that question?

4. What is indigenous leadership development? What does it have to do with Christianity?

5. John tells the story of how his grandson is imagining a new kind of church. What is his grandson's vision? What visions do you have for a new kind of church?

6. What would need to change in your church for authentic relationships to flourish?

Chapter 5: God's Movement in the Twenty-First Century

1. Charles learns from Mark Gornik that we can't be fully Christian if we are culturally isolated. How is this true?

2. If the church is to be an alternative social reality, what does this new way of living together look like? How does it look different from, yet exist in the midst of, the larger society?

3. Charles writes on page 97, "We don't need to shout the gospel louder than competing messages so much as we need to learn to be quiet in a noisy nation." Why is silence vital to Christian living? How might you live a more contemplative life?

4. On pages 101-2 Charles makes a case for Christians participating in interfaith partnerships to work for justice. How are

interfaith relationships a matter of humility?

5. "Friendship across the dividing lines of our society may be the best chance we have of relearning the language of peace" (p. 106). Why is friendship across dividing lines so much more difficult than service across dividing lines? What does this sort of friendship require?

6. Where, if any, are the spaces in your life where such friendships are flourishing? How can you pursue such friendships?

CHAPTER 6: A TIME FOR REBUILDING

1. On page 111, John asks, "What does the church have to offer a community where healthy men beg on the street corner?" How would you answer that question with respect to your church and your community?

2. How do our courts and jails reflect the brokenness of our society? In what specific ways are we called to interrupt the brokenness of those systems?

3. How does God's blessing work? What is our role in receiving blessing? What is God's role?

4. How can you invest in your community? How can your church invest in the community it is in? Are you located in the neighbor-

hood to which God has called you?

5. What do you have too much of? What are you lacking? How is your stuff serving the God movement? How is your stuff hindering your participation in God's work?

6. John explains how personal formation is crucial to the larger movement of reconciliation and community development. How is your church investing in personal formation? Where are your personal strengths in discipleship? Where do you need help and formation?

7. What have you learned from reading this book? How is God leading you to join in God's movement?

Acknowledgments

CHARLES

When someone calls you up on the phone and says, "God has a plan for your life and I know what it is," your first inclination should probably be to hang up and consider changing your phone number. This was my temptation when Chris Rice contacted me a couple of years ago to say God wanted me to write this book. He didn't ask me to write it, or coax me with flattering remarks. He said flatly that God wanted me to write it.

To be sure, the prospect of collaborating with my dear friend, confessor, hero and mentor John Perkins sounded like a wonderful invitation. But there were so many other obligations and unmet deadlines on my desk—and then of course Chris's irritating Bill Bright impersonation. Couldn't we have this conversation later?

Still, what made the phone call most vexing was that I knew from the first moment that Chris (and/or God) was right. I've known Chris Rice for a long time. Spencer Perkins introduced us over a meal of chicken and dumplings and collard greens in a Mississippi café on a hot summer day in 1993 when I was in the South on research. Over the years, I spent time with Chris and Spencer at Antioch, the interracial community in West Jackson where the Rices and Perkinses lived as "reconciliation partners" in a rambling old house open to anyone in need of a bed, a meal and a friend. Chris and I had hung out together at the thirtieth celebration of the 1964 Freedom Summer Project, and as he told me his story and shared his vision of community building, I began to think about the deep connections between the movement of the 1960s and the activism of contemporary Christian community builders. Those conversations would frame the argument of my book *The Beloved Community: How Faith Shapes Social Justice, from the Civil Rights Movement to Today.* Over the years, I have organized numerous adult education seminars around the evangelical classic Chris coauthored with Spencer, *More Than Equals: Racial Healing for the Sake of the Gospel,* and he's always been generous in sharing his story with my students. So I owed him one.

More importantly, however, I realized that the invitation to deliver a series of lectures and write a book with Dr. Perkins was a precious and unexpected gift. And so for this gift, and the privilege of offering my perspective on the "quiet revolution," I am exceedingly grateful not only to Chris but also to his colleague and codirector at the Duke Center for Reconciliation, the theologian and priest Father Emmanuel Katongole. What a rewarding experience this has been.

Heeding Chris's plan for my life has also enabled me to work closely with Jonathan Wilson-Hartgrove, who continues to provide brilliant editorial direction for the Resources for Reconciliation series. I have learned so much about reconciliation and peacemaking from Jonathan's own writings and from his ministry and life among the new monastics. I am blessed to be the beneficiary of his wisdom and supervision, and I look forward to many future exchanges with this creative young theologian.

One other acknowledgment is in order: fifteen years ago, while teaching together in the theology department at Loyola College in Baltimore, Greg Jones and I talked often of how the Christian vision of forgiveness and reconciliation might be incarnated in an institutional setting. Duke Divinity School has flourished in every respect as a result of Greg's leadership in the dean's office, but the Center for Reconciliation, a venture no doubt filled with many risks and challenges, stands in my mind as the capstone of Greg's theological vision. I am grateful to him for translating words into brick and mortar, and for creating a space in one of the world's most influential theological centers where reconciliation can be theologically articulated and translated into concrete strategies for global healing.

Finally, please check out our website, <www.livedtheology .org>, and help us shape the vision.

JOHN

Since he retired from teaching in 1994, Lowell Noble has been with me here in Jackson, Mississippi. He's eighty-two and I'm seventy-eight now, but whenever I get tired, all I have to do is have a conversation with Lowell about a biblical passage, and I'm reinvigorated. He's always reading what people are talking about, and he keeps me up to date. I'm so grateful for Lowell's friendship.

Relationships with people enrich your life. There have always been people older than me whom I respected, but who were also approachable. Those relationships have made me more than I could have been on my own. I'm glad to still have that kind of relationship with Lowell. But I'm older than most people I know now. Remembering the gifts I've received reminds me that we need to pass this on to others.

So Lowell and I have started offering retreats at the John M. Perkins Retreat Center here in Jackson. I'm so grateful for the relationships I've had over forty-eight years of ministry, and I'd like to invite you to come and experience the joy of this community we've found by God's grace. If you're interested in participating in one of our intimate, personal retreats, call (601) 354-1563 or visit <www.jmpf.org/content/leadership/retreat_center/>. I hope to see you here soon.

Notes

CHAPTER 1: THE UNFINISHED BUSINESS OF THE CIVIL RIGHTS MOVEMENT

[1]Clayborne Carson, "The Boycott That Changed Dr. King's Life," *New York Times Magazine*, January 7, 1996.

[2]Martin Luther King Jr., *Stride Toward Freedom: The Montgomery Story* (San Francisco: Harper & Row, 1983), pp. 121-22.

[3]Martin Luther King Jr., *The Autobiography of Martin Luther King Jr.*, ed. Clayborne Carson (New York: Warner Books, 1998), p. 78.

[4]Martin Luther King Jr., *The Papers of Martin Luther King Jr.*, ed. Stewart Burns, Susan Carson, Peter Holloran and Dana L. H. Powell (Berkeley: University of California Press, 1996), 3:136.

[5]Kwame Anthony Appiah, with Amy Gutmann, *Color Conscious* (Princeton, N.J.: Princeton University Press, 1998), p. 104.

[6]Stanley Wise, May 11, 1966, staff meeting, SNCC Papers, Martin Luther King Jr. Center, Atlanta, Georgia.

[7]"Assumptions About SNCC," SNCC Papers.

[8]John Herbers, *The Lost Priority: What Happened to the Civil Rights Movement in America?* (New York: Funk & Wagnalls, 1970), p. 207.

[9]See David Burner, "The Liberals' War in Vietnam," in *Making Peace with the Sixties* (Princeton, N.J.: Princeton University Press, 1996), pp. 189-216.

[10]Martin Luther King Jr., *A Testament of Hope*, ed. James M. Washington (San Francisco: HarperOne, 1990), p. 234.

[11]John Perkins and Thomas A. Tarrants, *He's My Brother: Former Racial Foes Offer Strategy for Reconciliation* (Grand Rapids: Baker, 1994), p. 133.

[12]John Perkins, *Radix*, March-April 1977, p. 7.

[13]John Perkins, *A Quiet Revolution: The Christian Response to Human Need, A Strategy for Today* (Pasadena, Calif.: Urban Family Publications, 1976), pp. 219-20.

[14]Ibid., pp. 140-41.

[15]Ibid., p. 220.

[16]Alan Boesak, *Black and Reformed* (Johannesburg, South Africa: Skotaville, 1984), p. 32.

[17]Credentials Committee Transcript, 1964, Joseph Rauh Papers, Library of Congress, Washington, D.C.

[18]John Perkins, "Stoning the Prophets," *Sojourners*, February 1978, p. 8.

[19]Perkins, *Quiet Revolution*, p. 35.

[20]Ibid.

[21]Ibid., p. 141.

[22]Timothy J. Gorringe, *Karl Barth: Against Hegemony* (Oxford: Oxford University Press, 1999), p. 49.

[23]John Perkins, *Let Justice Roll Down* (Ventura, Calif.: Regal, 1976), p. 218.

[24]Perkins, *Quiet Revolution*, p. 218. Perkins believed in capital ownership and always recoiled when members of peace churches proposed that Voice of Calvary implement the practice of the common purse. Voice of Calvary existed to foster black economic empowerment. The operations of free enterprise and redistribution of wealth through reparations could be brought to unity in prophetic Christianity.

[25]Ibid., p. 207.

CHAPTER 2: THE CULTURAL CAPTIVITY OF THE CHURCH

[1]For more information on CCDA, see <www.ccda.org> or attend our annual conference, hosted in a different U.S. city in the fall of each year.

[2]Eberhard Arnold, quoted in Peter Mommsen, *Homage to a Broken Man* (Rifton, N.Y.: Plough, 2004), p. 22.

Chapter 3: The Power of True Conversion

[1]Fannie Lou Hamer, "To Praise Our Bridges," in *Mississippi Writers: Reflections of Childhood and Youth,* ed. Dorothy Abbot (Jackson: University Press of Mississippi, 1984), 2:324.

[2]See my theological narrative of Mrs. Hamer in *God's Long Summer: Stories of Faith and Civil Rights* (Princeton, N.J.: Princeton University Press, 1997), pp. 10-48.

[3]Fannie Lou Hamer, cited in Edwin King, "Go Tell It on the Mountain," *Sojourners,* December 1982, p. 87.

[4]Henri de Lubac, *The Discovery of God,* trans. Alexander Dru (Grand Rapids: Eerdmans, 1996), p. 190.

[5]John Perkins with Jo Kadlecek, *Resurrecting Hope: Powerful Stories of How God Is Moving to Reach Our Cities* (Ventura, Calif.: Regal, 1995), p. 19.

[6]Lubac, *Discovery of God,* p. 159.

[7]Friedrich Nietzsche, *The Antichrist,* trans. Anthony M. Ludovici (New York: Prometheus, 2000), p. 70.

[8]Friedrich Nietzsche, *Thus Spake Zarathustra,* in *The Philosophy of Nietzsche* (New York: The Modern Library, 1940), p. 98.

[9]Victoria Gray Adams, lecture given at the Conference on Lived Theology and Civil Courage, University of Virginia, June 13, 2003.

[10]John Lewis, correspondence, March 1964, SNCC Papers, Martin Luther King Jr. Center, Atlanta, Georgia.

[11]Karl Barth, *The Word of God and the Word of Man,* trans. Douglas Horton (Gloucester, Mass.: Peter Smith, 1978), p. 286.

Chapter 5: God's Movement in the Twenty-First Century

[1]Diane Nash, from a lecture given at University of Virginia.

[2]As the African theologian John Mbiti observes, "The centers of the church's universality [are] no longer in Geneva, Rome, Athens, Paris, London, New York, but Kinshasa, Buenos Aires, Addis Ababa, and Manila" (John Mbiti cited in Philip Jenkins, *The Next Christendom: The Coming of Global Christian-*

ity [New York: Oxford University Press, 2002], p. 2).

[3]Daniel J. Wakin, *New York Times*, April 18, 2004.

[4]Mark Gornik, "Signs of the Spirit in the City," accessed February 13, 2006 <www.livedtheology.org/silt2005_session3_transcript.html>.

[5]Mark Gornik, interview with the author.

[6]Dietrich Bonhoeffer, *Christ the Center*, trans. Edwin H. Robertson (New York: Harper & Row, 1978), p. 27.

[7]Thomas Merton, "Letter written to James H. Forest, February 21, 1966," in *The Hidden Ground of Love: The Letters of Thomas Merton on Religious Experience and Social Concerns*, selected and ed. William Henry Shannon (New York: Farrar, Strauss and Giroux, 1985), pp. 294-95.

[8]Max Picard, *The World of Silence* (Wichita, Kans.: Eighth Day Press, 2002), p. 35.

[9]See the recent book by new monastics Shane Claiborne and Jonathan Wilson-Hartgrove, *Becoming the Answer to Our Prayers: Prayer for Ordinary Radicals* (Downers Grove, Ill.: IVP Books, 2008).

[10]Irenaeus, *Against Heresies*, ed. Alexander Roberts and James Donaldson (Grand Rapids: Eerdmans, 1989), p. 443.

[11]Ibid.

[12]Ibid.

[13]John Perkins, *A Quiet Revolution: The Christian Repsonse to Human Need, A Strategy for Today* (Pasadena, Calif.: Urban Family Publications, 1976), p. 223.

[14]Dietrich Bonhoeffer, *The Cost of Discipleship* (San Francisco: Harper Touchstone, 1995), p. 89.

[15]Dietrich Bonhoeffer, *Ethics*, trans. Neville Horton Smith (New York: Macmillan, 1955), p. 182.

[16]Thomas Merton, *Faith and Violence* (South Bend, Ind.: University of Notre Dame Press, 1968), pp. 142-43.

[17]Martin Luther King Jr. cited in Taylor Branch, *Pillar of Fire* (New York: Simon & Schuster, 1998), p. 30.

[18]Perkins, *A Quiet Revolution*, p. 223.

[19]See Ashley Diaz Mejias's moving tribute to Victoria Gray Adams (1926-2006), "Letter from Charlottesville," Arts & Sciences Online, University of Virginia, posted February 22, 2007 <http://aands.virginia.edu/x10030.xml>.

About the Duke Divinity School
Center for Reconciliation

Our Mandate

Established in 2005, the center's mission flows from the apostle Paul's affirmation in 2 Corinthians 5 that "God was in Christ reconciling the world to himself," and that "the message of reconciliation has been entrusted to us."

In many ways and for many reasons, the Christian community has not taken up this challenge. In conflicts and divisions ranging from brokenness in families, abandoned neighborhoods, urban violence and ethnic division in the United States to genocide in Rwanda and Sudan, the church typically has mirrored society rather than offering a witness to it. In response, the center seeks to form and strengthen transformative Christian leadership for reconciliation.

Our Mission

Rooted in a Christian vision of God's mission, the Center for Reconciliation advances God's mission of reconciliation in a divided world by cultivating new leaders, communicating wisdom and hope, and connecting in outreach to strengthen leadership.

OUR PROGRAMS

- Serving U.S. leaders through an annual summer Institute, gatherings, study weeks and workshops
- African Great Lakes Initiative serving leaders in Uganda, southern Sudan, eastern Congo, Rwanda, Burundi and Kenya
- Annual Teaching Communities Week featuring leading practitioners and theologians
- In-depth formation in the ministry of reconciliation through residential programs at Duke Divinity School
- Teaching Communities apprenticeships in exemplary communities of practice
- Resources for Reconciliation book series
- Visiting Practitioner Fellows

HOW YOU CAN PARTICIPATE

- *Pray for us and our work.*
- *Partner financially with the center.*
- *Join the journey.* Whether you are a student, pastor, practitioner, ministry leader or layperson, the center wants to support you in the journey of reconciliation. Explore our website and see how we might connect. <http://www.dukereconciliation.com>